Winter Comes,
Spring
OVERCOMES

Winter Comes, Spring OVERCOMES

Hope for Hurting People

Bill Henegar

Trilogy Christian Publishers A Wholly Owned Subsidiary of Trinity Broadcasting Network 2442 Michelle Drive Tustin, CA 92780

For information about special discounts for bulk purchases, please contact Trilogy Christian Publishing.

Trilogy Disclaimer: The views and content expressed in this book are those of the author and may not necessarily reflect the views and doctrine of Trilogy Christian Publishing or the Trinity Broadcasting Network.

Manufactured in the United States of America

10 9 8 7 6 5 4 3 2 1

Library of Congress Cataloging-in-Publication Data is available.

B-ISBN#: 978-1-64773-400-8

E-ISBN#: 978-1-64773-401-5

To the special women in my life

Ruth Smith Henegar

Laurette Sirois Henegar

Patricia Morgan Henegar

Rebecca Henegar Moonen

Thank you for showing me
the Way more perfectly.

Introduction

If you have ever experienced pain or sorrow, if you have ever suffered from betrayal or loneliness, then it's you to whom I want to speak. I'm sure you know that the earth is filled with evil and sadness, but be sure that it's also filled with God's infinite love —and with His Spirit of life and restoration.

The earth is enveloped in the caring arms of our Creator. He knows your name and knows everything about you, from your infancy to your adulthood. And He's in love with you. I want to encourage you to open your heart and fill your mind with God's goodness as you read on. He wants the very best for you.

God carefully crafted you and me, and He wants us to have a good life and live with Him *forever*. I know I haven't said everything perfectly in this book, but I hope you will hear my heart: I genuinely want you to have *real Life* and have the illumination that comes only from God's *perfect Light*. The darkness is deep around us. But the Lord's Light will enable us to see beyond the evil that tries to deceive us, the evil that we may be experiencing at this very moment.

So, settle back into the peace of Jesus. He offers us *His own peace*—a peace we can find nowhere else. Soak in His forgiveness. Receive His great power. Let's think about the end of winter and the first tender sprouts of spring as the earth begins to warm.

Table of Contents

1

The Coming of Winter

It is with trepidation and caution that I begin this writing. Trepidation because only God has the answers to all our hurts and fears. Caution because I'm sure there are many things I will not know or be able to communicate to you. But because of the critical need, I'll press on.

A few years ago, I began thinking about all the pain and anguish, all the loneliness and fears that surround all of us. Suddenly, it was as if God opened my eyes to the tremendous needs that swirled around me. I nearly felt swallowed up with those painful needs. I was overwhelmed with the persuasiveness of suffering—in Africa, in Asia, in Europe and in the Americas. I thought of the billions of people who struggle daily against staggering challenges.

About a year ago, my friend John McCranie asked me to travel to his church in central California and speak on the subject of suffering and loss. His church had experienced many setbacks: beloved leaders had died, people suffered the loss of their soul mates, others were struggling with chronic pain and disability. In short, the church was being hammered with a whole array of discouraging situations, both individually and collectively. The church was sort of "shell shocked" (or experiencing PTSD). People felt under attack. And for all John knew, it was indeed a satanic attack on the potential of that fine church.

Reluctantly I agreed to go to present three messages in the same day: "Winter Comes," "God is Always the Answer" and "Spring Overcomes." I would love to say that my messages were the cure to the needs of that church, and that my lessons helped the church turn the corner. But as I left to drive home to southern California, I sensed that I had failed. Although there were some people who seemed to have been helped, many (perhaps most) were exactly where they were when I began to speak.

On the way home, something gripped me. I decided that a book was needed to say all the things I had failed to say, the encouragement that I had sought to be. For a year now, I've known I needed to put something on paper to those who might be encouraged. But something has held me back. Now, I begin these thoughts in the hope that I can say something that will turn your heart toward the One Who genuinely cares for you, the One Who has proved it over and over.

Winter Comes to Every Life

I'm not under the false assumption that this book will now answer all the unanswered questions about pain and suffering. Many great authors have written helpful books that do tremendous service to people who are hurting. But, somehow, I feel obligated to try to speak on the subject from my perspective and do my part in the war against suffering and loss. It occurred to me that *God Himself* is wanting to be the answer to our failures, fears, and afflictions.

This I know: winter comes to every life. And by "winter," I mean difficult seasons of life when we're buffeted by despair or pain, whether in body, mind or spirit. There could be *many* winters that come against us. No one is immune to discouragement, or suffering, or feelings of failure. Sometimes we bounce back quickly. But at other times, pain, in its various forms, lingers on and on, debilitating us, flattening us. And we are immobilized. What do we do at that point? That's what I want to explore in the next few chapters.

Winter usually comes suddenly—although it can gradually creep up on us. First, there's a chilly breeze that eventually stiffens into a bone-freezing wind. The cold increases until we are frozen into inaction and our spirits are stiff and unresponsive. This is the ugliness of life, the underbelly of peace and joy. Is God interested in that part of our life, or is He only interested in our peaceful and satisfying times? It's clear from His communication, His Holy Word given to us, that He's interested in every part of our life; He sees every tear and is concerned about every aspect of our welfare. He is, after all, a loving Father who wants the very best for us.

But what do we do when the cold of winter sets into our soul?

Perhaps, the first thing we should do in those circumstances is to acknowledge it and not try to ignore or hide from the negative realities and feelings. Even in difficult times—*especially* in the extremely difficult times—God wants to be near us and hear from us. Winter has a nearly endless variety of setbacks to use against us: the death of a loved one, disability, the loss of a job, divorce, betrayal, deepening debt, severe illness, physical or mental abuse...on and on the list continues. What's your setback? You can be assured that you are not the first to suffer that particular blow. And you won't be the last. Others have faced the winter you're facing. And they have overcome. So can you.

King David endured many "winters." When he was boy, he was overlooked and ridiculed by his older brothers. Later, when David was assigned to minister to King Saul, the king hated him and tried to kill him. Saul hunted the young man from village to cave, but God delivered David. Later, when David became king, he was caught in adultery and the plot to kill his lover's husband. As king, he endured a terribly dysfunctional family of spoiled children. At the end, he faced illness when he was alone. But nevertheless, David's wonderful psalms are evidence that he didn't allow those "winters" to define him or destroy him.

My Story

Why do I presume to address the problems of suffering and pain? I've traveled the weary road of life's reversals before many of you (because of my age). I don't know everything about pain and suffering, but I do know some things. There are experts in nearly every field in life, but no one is an expert in suffering. There are NO PhDs in pain. Yes, there are those who have studied the "phases" or "stages" of grief and discouragement, and there are experts in coping skills for fighting back failure. But the only ones to whom we should look concerning dealing with pain and sorrow are those who have overcome the challenges—and have found some answers regarding dealing with setbacks.

I tell you my own story, not for sympathy, but to illustrate my qualifications to speak of suffering. As I grew up, I had to deal with the dark uncertainties of World War II. My father joined the war effort in Germany and France, so my mother and I were alone to face the threats to world peace. Money was always scarce, and we had to deal with the government's rationing of many essentials.

I remember being told by my teachers, "Do not pick up any brightly colored pieces outside that appear to be candy. They might be tiny bombs meant to maim your hand or face, floated to California by the enemy." My mother and I would sit by the radio and listen to the news from the frontlines of battles in Europe and Asia and the Pacific Islands. I remember it as a time of eerie quiet in the neighborhood. And I remember the small banner in the window of our neighbor across the street, a blue banner with a gold star. That meant that home had a serviceman who wouldn't be coming home.

Finally, when my father returned from the war after victory was won, the "war" actually continued in our home. He became a raging alcoholic, trying to deal with what he had experienced on the front lines. It compounded the trouble of his own childhood.

So, our house was often a war zone of its own. My father had lost his father, whom he idolized, when he was just thirteen. So that trauma was deepened by the scenes of war. He would often go into spells of depression and drink alcohol to anesthetize the memories. For days on end he would be in a drunken stupor and couldn't work.

When I was seven, our family began to grow: a brother was added, then a sister. Later, two more brothers joined the family. My junior high and high school days were strained to say the least. I couldn't invite my friends to my home because of fear of what my father might do. In addition, my father often lost so much work that my mother, and myself at age 16, had to work outside the home to make a meager living. So, my home life affected my school and social life. When I was eighteen, I joined the U.S. Air Force, in many ways to escape my home life.

When I was discharged from the Air Force, I married a beautiful and wonderful girl I had met in Maine where I was stationed for more than three years. She became my true soul mate, and we had a blessed life together. I also discovered Christ as Lord and Savior at age 23, though God had been drawing me to Him from childhood. Laurette also became a Christian at the same time as me. Then 46 years later, after raising our family of three boys and a girl, Laurette died from breast cancer. She had become the heart, the very center of our family, so her loss was devastating to us all. In the same year that she died, my sweet mother also died, as did a favorite uncle and the mother of my sister-in-law. 2005 was "a bitter winter" that closed in around me with a freezing grip. Sensing futility, I retired from my rewarding career of more than 32 years at Pepperdine University in Malibu. I was all alone and defeated.

Consolation

Surprisingly, a year and a half later, I was introduced to a Christian woman, Patricia Morgan, who had also lost her mate. She had been alone for 14 years and thought she would never find love again. We were brought together by a mutual friend, and, as she put it, "it was a God thing!" We nearly immediately fell in love and were married in November 2006. I told her, "We are not young anymore, so we will have to cram a lot of living into ten years." And we did indeed! We traveled to England and Ireland and places across America. We were gloriously happy. But the last two of our twelve years together were painful, as she suffered terribly with ovarian cancer. In December 2017, she succumbed. And once again, I was left alone.

Along my journey, I had various health issues that plagued me, times of pain from chronic prostatitis, kidney stones, diabetes, and kidney failure. But I continued to set my future on God and praise Him for His great goodness. I'm convinced that the worst suffering comes from the feeling that God has abandoned us, that He doesn't know or care about our suffering. In other words, the worst suffering comes from within, from paralyzing fear. But that is an evil, deceptive lie. Jesus and many of the writers of the Bible admonished us to "fear not." Is it even possible to fear not? A better understanding of that teaching might be, "Go ahead, move forward and ignore the fear! Don't let fear control you." Joyce Meyer says, "Do it afraid!"

I tell you my story so that you won't think my life has been all bright days and roses without thorns. I've had my share (or more than my share) of trials and tribulations: losing mother, father, two wives, relatives and friends, growing up in troubled times and a dysfunctional family, not to mention my health issues. But through it all, I have been able, by God's grace, to look back and rejoice at what the Great Father has done for me. From the time I was just a little boy, God seemed to speak to me and lead me. Till this very day, I've sensed the Father's presence—perhaps even His pleasure. So, I can say without equivocation, God is near to those who call on Him.

We simply must believe, for survival sake, that God is *not* a sadist; He doesn't enjoy our misery. It's important to know and believe that WE ARE NOT ALONE in this world, and the Lord is not responsible for our pain. God is there, with us all the way. He'll help us. And winter will eventually end. A brighter day is coming. In fact, we should have faith that God is a Good Father and wants the very best for us. Bad times come to all of us and test us. The question is: Will we stand? As life grows darker, we must seek God more earnestly to strengthen us. My friend Daniel Jolliff has said, "If you must suffer, make sure you get something from it." In other words, don't endure the pain without any gain!

We must know this: we're not being singled out by God. He doesn't "have it in for us." We are not unique, even though we might like to think we are. Actually, our losses are doing something in us; they are changing us. Will the changes be for better, or worse?

Though we don't often think about it, life begins in pain. Long ago, our original mother, Eve, was cursed with pain in childbirth. Our own mothers experienced that same pain as we entered the world. So, what's the first thing a baby does after the mother's pain in childbirth? It cries! *It's the pain of transition.* And the pain continues; we hurt all through life as we go through transitions. God never promised us we'd be kept from harm. But He did promise us He would be with us *through* the harm. Remember, Jesus Himself had to experience great pain. And he had to endure hatred, injustice, abuse, rejection, and a life that culminated in excruciating death. He understands our pain and sorrows. So, pain is a part of life. But only we can make it the dominant part of life.

Long ago, humanity went astray, declaring in effect, "I'll do it my way." How small and twisted are our arrogant ways! How short sighted! Our condition today is not God's fault, but the fault of our ancestors who set the trajectory for the failures of future generations. Humanity's rejection of God many centuries ago was the first step away from perfection, and we've been walking farther away ever since.

Interesting, isn't it, that many animals have something we call "instinct"? We can't see instinct or measure it, but we know it's there. I heard about a certain cave in Africa where elephants go in the middle of the night to lick salt from the walls and ceiling of the cave. They seem to have a "memory" of the cave, even if they've never been there before. Instinct drives them many miles to this special place. Is it the salt? No one knows why they travel so many miles to go there. It seems to be supernatural. But we humans reject any "instinct" in our being, because we have "reasoning." Elephants too have reasoning to a lesser degree. But the elephants pay attention to their instincts, nevertheless. What supernatural instincts do we have that we may be ignoring? Many have postulated that we have an inner instinct to search for our heavenly Father.

Seems reasonable to me!

I'll share with you one of the most important lessons I've learned in my long life. Robert Morris once said something like the following: "The Bible is a supernatural book, written to supernatural people, and only supernatural people can truly understand it." When I heard that, I thought, "That's the conclusion my life has been moving toward for many years!" I've spent many decades analyzing and rationalizing the word of God. But in the last part of my life, I've decided to simply read it and believe it. No more human reasoning for me; it's only taken me down a dead-end. For me, I choose to have faith alone.

God Understands

From my reading of the Scripture, I believe God understands our pain and our losses of all kinds. What's more, I believe God entered our earthly realm to experience our human senses of sorrow, suffering, and even shame. God didn't ignore the ancient man named Job, who suffered the loss of nearly everything: his considerable possessions, family, friends and his own health. God's answer to Job's suffering was not indifference, but it was to redirect Job's attention away from himself and to the Maker of all things. After all, this life, even at its longest, is brief and passes quickly. It's been famously said, "It's not about you." I certainly agree with that, but at the same time, *it is about you!* God loves you more passionately than you can imagine. After all, you are His beloved child. He created you and gifted you with talent and potential. It's not that you are the center of the universe. God alone is in that exalted position. But He wants you to be His friend, His child, His delight. But it all begins with acknowledging Him as God and Father. Only then can you truly become His beloved son or daughter.

In the case of the ancient patriarch, Job, God answered Job's desire for intimacy. The Lord understood his plight (had always understood it), and eventually God restored everything to him. Job received restoration in his life. But sometimes our restoration is found *beyond* this present life, in God's home country. Are we willing to wait? Do we have confidence that there's a "cave" somewhere that satisfies all our instinctive desires?

I invite you to pour your heart out to God. Tell Him about your pain, your disappointments, your failures—your bitter winters. He can take your complaints. Then think of all that you have both now and in the past. Praise Him. A Father wants to be acknowledged and loved. God will take your praise. He will also take your misgivings, your accusations, even your railings against Him. But don't stop there. Seek His face, not that you can see His face (if you were to see His face you would surely die), but you can, and should, seek His wonderful *presence!* Draw near to Him and He will draw near to you, to comfort and heal.

There is a Hebrew word, *Aliyah*, that means "going up" or "ascending." Today it's used of those Jews who leave the place where they've been displaced and have traveled to Israel, to the true home they've never seen. However, long before it was used in that sense, *Aliyah* was familiar to Jews of many past centuries as the journey upward to the temple in Jerusalem. Psalm 120 through Psalm 134 in the Bible are called the "songs of accents." They're songs that were to be sung by pilgrims as they went up to the higher elevations of the temple mount and the courts of the Lord. The concept is exciting and expansive. It's like the journey we all are on, going higher and higher toward the Father. In our pain, we should try to remember to sing songs of ascension. We are going upward. We are going higher. Do you think God is pleased if we sing to Him as we're marching upward toward Him? You know He is!

One of those songs of ascent is Psalm 130. I suggest you read it and dedicate it to God. It may be the confidence you need to endure:

Out of the depths I cry to you, O LORD;

O LORD, hear my voice.

Let your ears be attentive to my cry for mercy.

If you, O LORD, kept a record of sins,

O LORD, who could stand?

But with you there is forgiveness; therefore you are feared.

I wait for the LORD, my soul waits, and in his word I put my hope.

My soul waits for the Lord more than watchmen wait for the morning,

more than watchmen wait for the morning.

O Israel, put your hope in the LORD,

for with the LORD is unfailing love and with him is full redemption.

He himself will redeem Israel from all their sins.

Winter comes to every life at one time or another. Perhaps you are in the middle of a chilling winter right now. But listen: you can rise up today! Wait for the Lord, as we read in the psalm above. Rise up and put your hope in the Lord Jesus because of His unfailing love. With Him, is full redemption!

2

Wave After Wave

From many experiences, I know that you and I struggle to breathe and survive when pain and circumstance crash in on us. It's like losing our balance as we're wading in the ocean, stumbling down under the surf. As we scramble to our feet, an unexpected second wave hits us, and down we go again. Then just about the time we catch our balance, yet another wave knocks us down. Wave after wave. This is what many of us experience. Those waves of difficult times are involuntary; they're not our fault. They're not brought on by our own self-consciousness. They seem to have a life of their own, a desire to see us scrambling for breath.

When we come up for air and suck in that precious oxygen, we're momentarily alive. But not for long. Another wave swamps us, and we're struggling again. What are these repetitive waves? They are waves of pain or discouragement. They might be the loss of someone very dear to us that sinks us. Or they might be the loss of a job or a career. They may be some past regret or shameful memory that keeps coming back to haunt us. Whatever the cause, they are successive waves of disappointment and pain. These waves come one upon another. The bottom line is, the repetitive nature of them wears us down. The loss of a loved one can produce powerful waves of grief; illness can bring withering waves of pain. Other setbacks can cause rolling waves of regret or painful memories. You fill in the blank of the cause.

In the physical sense, the only way to avoid the waves is to get out of the surf. We must determine to deal with the problem or set of problems. Avoidance only prolongs the pain. Allow me to say that if it's physical pain you are suffering with, you must seek medical help as soon as possible. Some people try to ignore pain and courageously press on. But that may not be courage; it may simply be stubbornness. Dealing with chronic pain is a serious problem that many people confront on a daily basis. We must be careful about self-medication, even though pharmaceuticals are urged on us by countless advertisements. Self-medication is usually not a good idea. A wiser solution is to seek professional medical help. If one professional doesn't have an answer, perhaps another one will.

But I'm talking here of something other than *physical* pain and suffering. The enemy—Satan—flashes memories into our mind and, often, it's the repetition that actually discourages us. One event may be survivable, but successive playback of events wears us down, weaken us. It's best to deal with the early waves and not wait until repeated waves hit us and swamp us. Fighting wave after wave will eventually tire us physically and emotionally, and then we have to deal with fatigue in addition to the original problem.

Most of the suffering we endure is involuntary, coming whether we welcome it or not. At the first wave of discouragement, we should cry out to God, "Help me, Lord! Help me!" If the pain is emotional anguish, perhaps we can even declare, "No, I won't go there, Lord. Help me to overcome this attack from the Evil One." Then we should set our mind on positive thoughts (I would suggest scripture, which is God's words to us) or encouraging images or music. And remember to seek God's peace. It's imperative that we break the cycle early, get rid of the toxic mood before the waves repeat. In many situations, it's possible to control our thoughts before they get us completely down.

When the Mind Wanders

I have found that my mind occasionally takes me to unwanted places where I despair and pity myself and my circumstances. It's not helpful to ask the air, "Why is this happening to me? What does it mean? When will it end?" Instead, thank God that He has blessed you at other times in your life, and pray that the spring will soon come. Don't ask, "Why?" Call for God to help you get your mind under control.

To shake off those unwanted questions, I begin by trying to identify those thoughts as coming from Satan and his demons. Do I really believe that all my thoughts are from my *own* mind? Isn't it possible that the enemy wants me to believe negative things, discouraging things that steal my peace? I simply can't give in to the enemy; instead, I must resist him—do my best to cast him out of my mind. Many of the attacks you and I experience are not only psychological, but they are also spiritual or supernatural. If that seems to be the case, get out of the surf! Expose the attack for what it is, an attack from outside of us by the enemy of our soul. Beware of people, even well-meaning friends (or evil entities) that want to bring you down and steal your peace. Force them away from you by repeatedly calling on God.

Many years ago, my wife Laurette and I went to a popular Mexican resort beach on vacation. As we waded in the water, she turned her back for a moment and a wave caught her by surprise. She tumbled over and under the water. I reached out and quickly caught her as she floundered, and she was fine. That example teaches me that sometimes we need a friend to reach out and help us. Be ready to ask for help in dealing with pain, disappointment and depression. It's very possible that others have experienced what you're facing. They may be able to offer help to you. Don't swim alone.

How can we "get out of the water" when the surf gets rough? In other words, how can we escape the repetition of debilitating thoughts that capture our mind—those pounding waves that pull us under?

Be Prepared

I don't have all the answers to defeating pain and fear, but here's what I have found. A place to begin is to *be prepared* for the mental attacks that will probably come our way. Don't turn your back to the waves! Understand they will come and be ready for them. But how is that possible since we have defined the attacks as unexpected? First of all, we can be ready for the attacks by arming ourselves with *faith* and *confidence* in God! Faith in God and confidence in His power and love can accomplish more than we may imagine. Faith and confidence can prevent that surprise attack. And faith can actually heal us emotionally if we are caught by a wave of discouragement— faith can even heal us physically! God tells us to cast all our burdens on Him because He cares for us. Some of us have heard that idea before, but we have not gotten the truth down in our spirit. At the very least, faith and confidence in God certainly can prepare us to combat discouragement and depression.

Depression is a long spiral downward. Many times, the cure is a long spiral upward, one small success at a time. But for people with strong faith, the upward journey can be rapid.

We can arm ourselves with faith and be confident in the extraordinary *love of God*. I suppose you would expect a writing like this, from a Christian perspective, to say such a thing. But what if that is actually true? What if God's love for us really is more profound than we can even imagine? Sometimes we need to turn our little belief into a deeper and more profound trust. What do we have to lose by trusting God? Is your life without Him so much better than your life with Him? What if these spiritual or supernatural acts, like placing our faith and confidence in God, can actually change something *in the spiritual realm* that affects our lives *in this natural world* and in our physical lives?

Another very powerful way to arm ourselves against the repetitive waves of pain and discouragement is to choose to be *thankful*. I've learned that thankfulness is a great antidote that can combat the poison of suffering. Once again, I'm not thinking so much of physical pain, of course, although even that may be alleviated to some extent by thankfulness. With the loss of both Laurette and Patricia, I learned that my anguish was greatly diminished when I began thanking God for His gift of the two precious wives He gave me. I thanked Him for the wonderful 46 years that He gave me with Laurette, for the four children she bore me, and for the way she made my life full and complete.

When Laurette passed, Patricia became a tremendous consolation. But then Patty also passed away. God, in His mercy, helped me to thank Him for the 12 years we had together, for the happiness that returned to my life in the last two decades. Actually, my heart began to overflow with gratitude so that I never became bitter or resentful for my loss. Periodical waves came, of course, but they didn't swamp me. The gratitude took away the sting of loss. Today, I certainly miss both the loves of my life. But I've realized more acutely that my greatest companion and deepest love ... is *God Himself!* He has promised to be with me forever.

We can also arm ourselves with *hope*, a little word with a profound promise and impact. Hope is an offspring of faith and love for God. We sometimes openly, or secretly, tend to blame God for our problems and ailments. We even call terrible things "Acts of God." Nothing could be farther from the truth. God is not the author of the bad things that happen in life. He is the *answer* to our problems and ailments. But as usual, Satan blurs the lines and reverses the truth so that white becomes black, and black becomes white. But the true One, Jesus, said, "The thief [Satan] comes only to steal and kill and destroy." But then He adds, "I have come that they [we] may have life, and have it to the full" (John 10:10). *Jesus is all about life.* Satan is all about death. We should try to remember that when we are assaulted by pain, loss, and suffering.

When the waves come roaring at you, be ready. Be prepared. Brace yourself *spiritually* against the force of the wave. Too often we think only in natural terms. But it's the *spiritual things* that are eternal, that are lasting. When I think of my mother, Ruth, who also went to be with the Lord in 2005, I remember her steadfastness and her faith, her quick and infectious laugh, and, most of all, the love she lavished on all her children and grandchildren. Those are the lasting impressions of her, *spiritual qualities* that linger long after the memory of her face fades away.

To my shame, I must admit that when Laurette was tumbled in the surf in Mexico, I had to laugh. I knew I could reach and grab her, so I wasn't worried about her. I immediately jumped to her side and held her tight. But I should not have laughed. She was embarrassed and irritated with me. And I don't blame her. I'm glad our God never laughs at our weakness and missteps. He understands our powerlessness. It's not as if He *inherited* us; it was He who *created* us—every molecule of us. He understands us perfectly. Life is a precious gift from our creator, and we must not squander it by floundering in the waves.

Psalm 103:13, 14 has a passage that has greatly encouraged me. It says, "As a father has compassion on His children, so the LORD has compassion on those who fear him; for He knows how we are formed, He remembers that we are dust." What is the passage getting at? It tells us that God is like any father who has compassion on his children. He understands that humans are weak and immature. But the passage goes on to say that God "knows how we are formed"—it was He who formed us, after all. Then the Bible says, "he remembers that we are dust." God knows that we are not of the same "substance" as He; we are simply the dust of the earth, from which He formed us, as it tells us in Genesis 2:7. He doesn't hold us to standards to which we can never attain. He knows us better than we know ourselves.

Another Strategy

A strategy for preparedness to counter the waves of discouragement is to arm ourselves with *prayer*. This may sound very weak to you, but don't be fooled. Prayer is a hot line to heaven, and God answers the phone Himself! We can't visit heaven (yet!), but we can get a message through to the Creator of the universe. We can pray *against* our enemy Satan. Jesus taught us to pray, saying, "… lead us not into temptation, but deliver us from the evil one" (Matthew 6:13). It was one of only a few things Jesus told us to pray about. He was concerned that we do combat with the devil. (Yes, the devil is real and active in our world.) Jesus Himself often warned us of the reality of Satan and his destructive work among us. So, we should come against Satan through the avenue of prayer.

There's another way of escaping the rolling, dangerous waves of discouragement—and that is to turn our pain and loss *upside down*. How? By using those difficult circumstances as a reminder to *pray for others*. It's amazing how thinking about and praying for others settles those waves of despair. Try it. Don't be unaware that Satan uses those emotional sieges against us to swamp us. But you can turn that whole situation into a powerful time of reaching out to others, through prayer. This is how God moves us to be concerned about those who may have even bigger problems than ourselves.

Periods of pain and loss can bring to mind important lessons for us. For example, we can pray, "God, this is a really difficult time for me, but I want to know if there is something you want me to learn and others you want me to reach out to and help." I hope you know that God doesn't deliberately bring troubled times into our lives. He's not trying to punish us or send us messages. However, even though He's not the instigator of those painful seasons, He can turn troubling times on their head and use them to teach us powerful truths.

King David suffered the loss of one of his sons, Absalom. The young man plotted against his father, the king, to overthrow him and become king in David's place. But even though Absalom conspired against his father, when the news came that Absalom had been killed, the king was filled with grief. David went away to be alone and wept, crying out, "O my son Absalom! My son, my son Absalom! If only I had died instead of you—O Absalom, my son, my son!" (2 Samuel 18:33).

David knew his son was against him and in the midst of a coup. Still, grief overtook him like an ocean wave and engulfed him. He even wished that he himself had died instead of his son Absalom. Grief may be irrational, but nevertheless, it simply exists and threatens to sink us. I remember when my wife Laurette died, I cried out, "O Laurette, why did you have to leave?" It was an irrational response. It was not her choice to die, but when grief engulfs us, reason goes out the window. All we know is that we hurt terribly. And God understands our emotions and our great sorrow. Don't forget that God faced terrible times when His people turned away from Him. We have every right to express our grief and pain. Eventually, the grief subsides and hopefully we return to our senses. It's at that point that we face an important choice: Do I move forward or do I lie in my misery from this point on? It's clear from Scripture that God would have us choose life!

Not long ago, I met a person who is especially remarkable. Her name is Helen Rhee. She was born in South Korea and moved to the U.S. when she was about 10 years old. While still in Korea, at about age 3, she contracted a rare infection. It worsened, and her left arm became twice its normal size. The doctors decided that the condition was incurable and that she wouldn't live more than a year or two. But the family called on the Christian community in Seoul, and thousands prayed for little Helen. Amazingly, she was healed! It was a great miracle, and her family claimed the blessing of God.

I wish that was the end of the story. But after she moved to America, Helen became ill again as a preteen. She suddenly began to suffer from fibromyalgia, severe arthritis, and other disabling diseases. But she continued her education, eventually earning a B.A. degree from the University of California, and both a master's degree and Ph.D. from Fuller Theological Seminary. She now teaches at Westmont College in Santa Barbara. She blesses many people, but she is still in constant pain.

She has never married nor done many of the things we take for granted. But she ministers weekly to others and encourages many through her speaking engagements. There's always someone worse off than us. But listen, I've never met anyone brighter, more humble or gentler than Helen Rhee. Sometimes God works through strange circumstances, but always to His glory and our good.

Can there be *purpose* in our suffering? There's an ancient Japanese artform called *Kintsugi*. When some people in Japan break a piece of pottery, they just throw it away. But others take their broken pottery to a very skilled artisan who puts the pieces together like a jigsaw puzzle. He puts the pieces back together with lacquered resin, then carefully paints the brokenness with powdered gold where the cracks had been. The finished piece is more beautiful *after* the breakage than *before*. Kintsugi is called "the art of precious scars." I believe God can do that for our lives, for our spirits—He can "make everything beautiful in its own time."

Faith and Confidence

The best defense against the wave after wave of despair is to be prepared. Don't let the succession of waves or the repeated discouragements take you by surprise. Expect those times and brace yourself against them. Face the waves with faith and confidence in the goodness of God. Be about the business of thanking God for His many kindnesses, despite your current situation. Allow the sweet salve of hope to heal your heart, knowing that in God's good time, He will bring comfort and healing—resurrection!—to your aching spirit. And there is available to us a great salve for the soul: conversation with God, or prayer. He hears us—He really does! This communication with the Father can change our condition and our outlook. When we pray, we should always remember to listen as well. Perhaps, God will speak to your heart in a special way at the very moment you need to hear from Him.

I saw a television documentary about some researchers that visited a village in Southeast Asia. The people of this village have a bizarre tradition of keeping their honored dead in the house with the family—not for a mourning period, but from then on! They often prepare a meal and present it to the embalmed body of their loved one as they visit the dead. And the documentary made me wonder, "Are we visiting the dead by rehearsing our troubles over and over? Can we get over our problems? Can we envision a new day and a new life?"

Satan tries to drag us under by taking us back to past failures. Some wonder, "Will this emptiness ever end?" It will end when we fill the emptiness with God's joy. Pain comes initially, but the real problem is when it repeats again and again. We must find a way out of the waves. We may think, "This pain is not fair!" But it's not about fairness. Fairness is taken care of in the Final Judgment. But in the surf, we should call out to God for grace! "Come, Lord Jesus, and rescue me from these waves."

Brace yourself. Get out of the water if you can. God is a miracle-working Father who loves you more than you will ever know. And He wants to heal you. He wants you to be at peace and at rest, without the oppressive feelings of abandonment, discouragement, and misery. Jesus said, "Peace I leave with you; my peace I give you. I do not give to you as the world gives. Do not let your hearts be troubled and do not be afraid" (John 14:27).

Believe it, and you will have it.

3

Take Heart

The words of Jesus are filled with encouragement: "In this world you will have trouble. But take heart! I have overcome the world" (John 16:33). Those two small words, *"take heart,"* change everything when they come from the Son of the Living God, and when they are embraced by ordinary people like you and me!

Jesus wants to convince us, "There is hope! Don't give up, because the story isn't finished. There is much more!" There's still more to be experienced, to be excited about and amazed at. Christ clearly had lived in the same corrupt world that we face daily, filled with evil and violence. His world of the first century may have been even more violent and dangerous than our own. He certainly was aware of our troubled and tortured world. He was the object of the world's hatred. Jesus was no Pollyanna.

So, He said to us, "In this world you will have trouble." How very true that is! We understand that truth and can join our stories of discouragement, loneliness and pain with those of the Lord. But Jesus had a *perspective* that we don't enjoy. He has a *viewpoint* we can never share, because He's aware of the world from an *eternal* perspective or viewpoint. He was and is the Alpha and the Omega, the beginning, and the end. What does that mean, exactly? It means that He was there at the very beginning of this world and the beginning of the whole universe—the beginning of everything we know or can imagine. He saw the first failure and the first murder. And He will be there at the very end of all things. When He finally says, "Everything's now fulfilled," and when He delivers the kingdom of heaven into the hands of His Father, that will be yet one more *new beginning*. He has far more invested in this world than we do. The world is precious to us, but far more precious to the Lord. He loves it with a passion, because He crafted it, then He redeemed it.

Because of His great love, the Lord Jesus is in our lives for the LONG TERM. Our thinking is always short term. It's the only way we can really think about things in this life. We're in "the moment." Our experience is confined to the here and now, and we can't see what the future holds; we can only vaguely understand the past. But Christ is NOT confined to this moment; He sees the beginning and the end—and everything between.

Thinking Back

When we're in elementary school, we play our role in our present experience; then when we enter high school, we may realize that elementary education was simply *preparation,* a platform for launching us into the next phase of our life. After that, we may move into college or into our working life, and again we realize that we had so little knowledge of the future. But it was preparation for the beginnings of adulthood. In other words, we obviously can only experience our present phase of growth and perhaps guess where our preparation might lead. But Jesus wants to be in our life for the *long term,* from beginning to end. He wants to move into our life and unpack His luggage and stay forever. He wants to be with us for preparation, for the various phases, and for the long term.

Usually, we are "short-term thinking people." We're pre-occupied with the next step. Or the one after that. "What's for lunch? What's for dinner? What's my next career move? What will I do in retirement?" Rarely do we wonder what is beyond our last breath. But Jesus is in this thing for the long haul. He says, "What will a person give in exchange for his soul?" (see Matthew 16:26). Where will you spend the rest of eternity? You won't simply vanish; you'll live on—somewhere.

We usually search for people to aid us in our journey, someone to be our coach or our helper to get us through to the next step. It might be a parent or a mentor or a friend or a lover. But Jesus Messiah steps up and says, "Surely I am with you always, to the very end of the age" (Matthew 28:20). That means, He is with us for the long term, through all our steps and phases. In fact, He is with us forever! Even though Christ journeyed back to His heavenly home, He didn't want us to feel like orphans. So, He asked God to send us a stand-in, a Counselor, something like Himself to be with us and to guide us through the steps, the phases, and chapters of our life. Holy Spirit is that lovely Counselor, representing Jesus our Savior.

What does it mean to have a long-term Counselor who will lead us through all of life and on into eternity? It should provide us with great *confidence* and *comfort* and relieve our mind. So, take heart in all the ups and downs of your life. View every downturn as simply a temporary setback. The apostle Paul says, "in all these things we are *more than conquerors* through him who loved us. For I am convinced that neither death nor life, neither angels nor demons, neither the present nor the future, nor any powers, neither height nor depth, nor anything else in all creation, will be able to separate us from the love of God that is in Christ Jesus our Lord" (Romans 8:37-39).

Does that mean God will always love us, regardless of our behavior? Yes. He may not approve of our behavior, but He will always love us and want the best for us. But it's important to acknowledge Him as your God and to depend on Him by faith. "Everything is possible for him who believes," said Jesus in Mark 9:23. If you love the Lord, you will want to please Him. Faith is the key that unlocks the future. Believe it and take heart!

Hope from Down Under

The talented Joel Houston of Hillsong Church in Australia wrote an encouraging song, "Take Heart," that's filled with meaning, and especially filled with hope:

> There is a light, It burns brighter than the sun
> He steals the night, And casts no shadow
> There is hope
> Should oceans rise and mountains fall, He never fails
>
> So take heart
> Let His love lead us through the night, Hold on to hope
> And take courage again, In death by love
> The fallen world was overcome, He wears the scars of our freedom
> In His Name, All our fears are swept away
> He never fails, So take heart
> Let His love lead us through the night, Hold on to hope
> And take courage again

The song goes on to speak of failure and fear, heartache and pain, burdens and shame, troubles and tears … and in all these challenges, "God our refuge, He has overcome." The inspiring song ends with: "God is with us, He has overcome, He has overcome."

There are those who consider themselves Christ-followers who can't bring themselves to believe the words above from Joel Houston. I know it's not easy to trust in Christ, but therein lies our true hope. Hope is in the believing.

Our enemy the devil wants to keep us doubting, discouraged and alone. What do we do when we pray and hear no answer? When God seems to be silent and our words to Him appear to bounce off the ceiling, what then? In that difficult time, I believe God is saying to us, "Take heart! Simply trust that I hear you, My child, and that the answer is on the way. Wait, and take heart."

I also believe it's imperative that we understand that we do indeed have a supernatural enemy, and that he wants to *destroy* us—or at least destroy our faith in the Lord. If we think the devil is simply a medieval fantasy, we'll not be aware when he tempts us or plants suggestive thoughts in our mind. If we don't understand that Jesus Himself actually did battle with the devil, we won't be able to distinguish between our thoughts, God's messages and the devil's perverse reasoning and temptations.

If we believe the Bible, it tells us that Jesus was led by Holy Spirit into the desert to be tempted by the very real devil, but the Lord was victorious over the Evil One (Matthew 4:1-11). It's that same devil that still speaks softly to us today with words of doubt and discouragement. To disguise himself, he used the personal pronoun, saying things like, "I am defeated. I can't go on. God is nowhere to be found. He won't help me. Besides all that, I'm not worthy for God to reach out to me, anyway." Those words sound like our own thoughts, so we embrace them. But they are lies. If we want the Truth, we must go to the Word of God. That's the only source of truth in the whole world.

"DIS-couragement" means to take away or steal a person's courage. Conversely, "EN-couragement" means to increase a person's courage, to lift them up. I'm amazed at how often we are willing pawns in the devil's hands. Inadvertently, we may steal away a loved one's or a friend's courage by some casual and unthinking comments. Or perhaps, we give our agreement to that person's pessimistic outlook. Over the past decades, I've tried to remind myself to speak encouragement to everyone I contact, even to strangers. It doesn't cost a thing, and the dividends are often enormous. So, we ought to remind ourselves to tell people, "Jesus says to take heart! He has overcome the world, and so can we!"

In ancient times, people set a certain period of time aside for mourning the loss of a loved one—or for getting over any challenge. In the case of a death, they even hired "professional mourners" to weep and wail, to help get beyond the period of mourning, because they were anxious to get back to life. In Ecclesiastes 3:4, it says, there is "a time to weep and a time to laugh, a time to mourn and a time to dance…". We can't help being thrust into despair at times. But God wants us to look ahead, to move on as soon as possible. To take heart.

If we refuse to take heart, we are denying Jesus' uplifting admonishment. He told us that we can become overcomers. But we have to choose to do so. If we'd rather sink into a pit of misery, then we'll "weep and mourn" from now on. But if we will reach out to the Lord, He will give us strength and courage to *take heart*—and move forward.

Entrusting Our Heart

We should entrust our heart to God. No matter the circumstances, He'll take good care of our heart. It's been noted that imprisoned people can be controlled in every way but one. Their movements can be limited. Their food can be determined. Every activity can be controlled. But no one can imprison the mind and heart of people. So, even if the devil is successful in controlling many circumstances in our life—things like health, companionship, mobility and more—he *cannot* control our heart. So, give your heart to the Lord. He will protect it and strengthen it. Ask God to guard your heart and mind. Philippians 4:7 reminds us, "And the peace of God, which transcends all understanding, will *guard your hearts and minds* in Christ Jesus."

The writer of Philippians, the apostle Paul, followed the statement above with a teaching on what we *should* be thinking about. We can, after all, control our own thinking. He said, "Finally, brothers, whatever is true, whatever is noble, whatever is right, whatever is pure, whatever is lovely, whatever is admirable—if anything is excellent or praiseworthy—think about such things" (Philippians 4:8). That list of "subjects to think about" is a far cry from what we see on television or the movies today. When I watch television today, I "channel-surf" to see what's being broadcast. And most often, I simply flip by the crime, sex, zombies, and materialism that dominate the airwaves.

The old adage applied to computers years ago is valid when applied to television today: Garbage in, garbage out. If we load our minds with programmed garbage, what do we expect to receive out of our minds? Still, our society shovels in the garbage by the boatload.

Psalm 119:28-31 says, "My soul is weary with sorrow; strengthen me according to your word. Keep me from deceitful ways; be gracious to me through your law. I have chosen the way of truth; I have set my heart on your laws. I hold fast to your statutes, O LORD; do not let me be put to shame." Rather than the "wisdom" of this world, we must choose to fill our mind with the Truth of God, our Maker.

In the verse that many consider the greatest in all Scripture, John 3:16, there are three truths that we must get down into the depths of our soul. Remember, this verse was spoken by the Son of God Himself. He was talking about His Father and about Himself. Those three truths are:

Number One: God loves us. Jesus said, "God so loved the world...." God doesn't just love us a little bit. He SO loved us—to the extent that He gave the most precious thing in all existence, His Son, to redeem us. We simply CANNOT forget that God loves us passionately.

Number Two: God suffered for us. Jesus said, "God gave His only son." Jesus was sacrificed for our sinfulness, not His own. Not only did Jesus suffer, but the Father suffered as He watched what His creation, lowly humans, were doing to His beloved Son. We may suffer, but God Himself suffered far, far more.

Number Three: God wants to save us. Jesus said, "God gave so we might not perish." The reason God was willing for His Son to die, and the reason Jesus was willing to go to the cross. was that you and I might have eternal life. That kind of love is totally amazing and extraordinary, and we are obligated to freely accept it.

I hope you'll remember those three things: God loves you; He suffered for you, and He wants you to be saved. He's not against you; He loves you so much!

We Have Choices

We like to feel that our choices are limited, that we are victims, "dry leaves blown by the wind." But this isn't true at all. Life is all about choices. We come to forks in the road, and we choose to go right or left. We always have choices, even when nearly all options are off the table. The choices of our mind are the "gatekeepers," and we control what we think about and what we allow into our conscience, and the direction we will go. When Joshua stepped up to lead the people of God after Moses died, God said to him, "As I was with Moses, so I will be with you; I will never leave you nor forsake you" (Joshua 1:5). Then God said, "Be strong and courageous. Do not be terrified; do not be discouraged, for the LORD your God will be with you wherever you go" (Joshua 1:9). God assumed (knew) the people had choices.

Earlier, God spoke to all Israel through Moses and said, "This day I call heaven and earth as witnesses against you that I have set before you life and death, blessings and curses. Now *choose life*, so that you and your children may live and that you may love the LORD your God, listen to his voice, and hold fast to him. For the LORD is your life, and he will give you many years in the land he swore to give to your fathers, Abraham, Isaac and Jacob" (Deuteronomy 30:19, 20). This passage shows us the heart of God. He wants us to be successful and live! But He gave us free will and we *must* choose.

Life is truly all about choices. And God risked everything and gave us freedom of choice: so, we can choose life or death, blessings or curses, good or evil. Even when we are discouraged and in the pit of misery, we still have choices to make. Because of the innate selfishness all of us face inside, we tend to turn inward and think only of our own welfare and what we believe we need in the moment. But take heart. God can help us reach outside our narrow life and step into His expansive life.

Jesus said, "I have overcome the world." He made that statement just a little while before He allowed evil men to nail Him to the cross. He was facing the painful end of His earthly life, but He could *still* claim victory! And how about us? Can we make the same claim? If we are IN CHRIST, then we can have victory in and through Jesus. He told us, "Peace I leave with you; my peace I give you. I do not give to you as the world gives. Do not let your hearts be troubled and do not be afraid" (John 14:27).

At times, we allow the peace Jesus gave us to slip through our fingers. It seems lost, and we struggle with fear. We cry, "God, where are you?" But He is where He has always been: At our elbow in the person of His Spirit. Jesus said that He didn't give us the earthly kind of peace, the peace that depends on all kinds of circumstances being just right. He called it "MY peace." That's the peace we should lay hold of! The Peace of Christ. He told us, in effect, Don't allow trouble to enter your heart. Keep it outside. Keep your heart pure and set on Me.

But how can Jesus ask us to NOT be afraid? We don't have control over fear, do we? No, fear is an involuntary or emotional response. We don't have control over our emotions, or external circumstances for that matter, but we can control our *reactions* to those circumstances. Remember that "Do not be afraid" means "Do whatever you are called to do and *do it afraid*." Don't let fear stop you from your faithful tasks.

Something to consider: Why should we "take heart," as we've suggested in this chapter? Because of one word: *Resurrection!*

What other religion or world view or philosophy elevates the word "resurrection" to such a high place? None. However, the whole of creation cries out the word and the concept.

This is the concept and *the reality* that changes everything! It changes not just a few things or most things, but everything!

All things pale in the light of the Sunday morning angel's message long ago, "He is not here; he has risen, *just as he said*" (Matthew 28:6). Jesus had told His followers that He would be killed, but that we would rise again! And it was *just as He said!* Take away the resurrection and the Christian religion collapses. It's all busy work if Jesus didn't walk out of that tomb. Skeptics and scoffers have tried to destroy the Good News for centuries. But they have failed, because Jesus lives. And because He lives, we too can live.

I'm amazed at how we can allow little things to obscure BIG THINGS. We can allow aches and pains, down-turns and loneliness, and many other reversals to get us down. But the glaring truth is, *Jesus lives!* So, what difference do our reversals ultimately make? Certainly, Jesus cares about our reversals, but He wants us to remember, down deep, that there is resurrection. That's why Paul told us that "we are more than conquerors," in Romans 8. Nothing should disturb the resoluteness of our spirits. We are *people of life* with confidence of the resurrection. So take heart!

One of the things that should keep us on track is the nurturing of our faith we receive through the years. Jesus told a dear friend who lost her brother, "I am the resurrection and the life. He who believes in me will live, even though he dies; and whoever lives and believes in me will never die" (John 11:25, 26). Then He turned to Martha and said, "Do you believe this?" He might well ask us the same question: "Do you indeed believe these things?" If we believe in Jesus and His resurrection, what can defeat us? The obvious answer is, *Nothing!*

So, whatever troubles us, or worries us, or gives us pain … in the brilliant light of Jesus' resurrection will not only be survivable, but also will be *conquerable*. We have the peace of

Christ within us.

So, "take heart," Jesus tells us. He has overcome life and death, the world's hatred, and the schemes of humans. He has, in fact, overcome the whole world. And with the help of our Savior, so can you and I.

4

The Peace of God

When we're stressed and worried, we often forget the most basic things, like the passage we just read at the end of chapter three (He who believes in me will live, even though he dies). When we have huge problems come our way, when pain or sorrow engulf us, when we're hurting from any number of conditions or situations, we often forget that God knew these things would happen to us. He's always known this from the very beginning of time, and He has made a way for us to be victorious over the world's attacks on our peace. With tremendous power, He provided for our escape from those hurtful things. We simply must believe that God loves us and wants the best for us. We shouldn't impute evil and pain to our God. He didn't create the world just to torture His own creation. But we do have an enemy who wants to do exactly that ... and blame it on God. That enemy is a liar, a thief, and a murderer.

It's not as though God was unprepared for the things that happen to you and me. Jesus, we're told, was "a man of sorrows, and familiar with suffering" (Isaiah 53:3). He came to earth on a dangerous rescue mission. And He was a real human being, with all the feelings, and sensitivities, and pains that we have. While He was on the earth, He was not immune to the weaknesses we endure. He understands the pressures and the pain of living in this fallen world. There's nothing we experience that He hasn't already experienced before us. He completely understands that the odds we face are sometimes against us.

Though it may be hard to believe, God's Spirit has already armed us with the internal power we need to combat all sorts of trials and losses if we are believers. The Spirit of God is perhaps the most misunderstood and least appreciated and utilized force (person) in life. He is God. He is not separate from God, nor is He some vague inanimate power. He is the Spirit of the Eternal God in Heaven, an extension of the Almighty into all the earth. If you are a follower of Christ, you have tremendous power in the person of the Spirit, of which you may be unaware.

When Jesus went back to heaven, Holy Spirit came at Jesus' request in order to empower us to live the lives to which He called us. The Spirit does for us what Jesus in the flesh could not do. Jesus was WITH His followers, but He could not be IN them because He was a true, physical person. Now Holy Spirit, representing Jesus, is IN those Christ-followers. What a difference! This concept was something the Old Testament prophets foretold. They prophesied that a time was coming when God would actually live inside us!

Ezekiel, for example, wrote,

> I will sprinkle clean water on you, and you will be clean; I will cleanse you from all your impurities and from all your idols. I will give you a new heart and put a new spirit in you; I will remove from you your heart of stone and give you a heart of flesh. And I will put my Spirit in you and move you to follow my decrees and be careful to keep my laws. You will live in the land I gave your forefathers; you will be my people and I will be your God. (Ezekiel 36:25-28).

This prophecy was given by God to Ezekiel more than 500 years before Jesus came upon the scene!

If we really believe Ezekiel's prophecy, how can we live defeated lives? How can we live in depression and hopelessness for prolonged periods? Ezekiel said the coming of the Spirit would happen, and *it did happen*, twenty centuries ago, when God sent Holy Spirit at the request of Jesus.

The best of friends and comforters here on this earth can comfort us for only a little while. They eventually must return to their own lives, their own families and their own problems. But God's great Comforter will NEVER leave us! He'll stay forever, unless we turn Him away. Even when winter repeatedly comes, He will remain. Give your suffering and pain to Holy Spirit.

The Spirit of Peace

Read the encouraging passage from the apostle Paul that follows: "Do not be anxious about anything, but in everything, by prayer and petition, with thanksgiving, present your requests to God. And the peace of God, which transcends all understanding, will guard your hearts and your minds in Christ Jesus" (Philippians 4:6, 7).

Now, you may have heard that passage before, or even carefully studied it. There are those who simply doubt that this admonition is literally true. It's a little too supernatural for many people. However, did Ezekiel and Paul know something that has escaped our modern understanding? What if you don't really have to worry? What if you can present your troubles and your requests to God with thanksgiving? What if the peace of God truly will guard your heart and mind in Jesus? Wouldn't that be remarkable? I believe Philippians 4 is not only possible, but is also a solemn promise from our gracious God.

Maybe, instead of struggling to understand Paul's statement, we should simply believe it and embrace it as coming from the Lord of the universe. We usually want "logical" explanations. We've become too locked into scientific inquiry and empirical data. If God is real, He knows the truth about how the universe works (He created it all!). And perhaps He wants us to simply obey what He tells us. If He really is the creator of the world, including us, He must know how everything was put together. He must know the source of the thing we call "peace." I believe, ultimately, only God can provide the peace that passes understanding, the peace we long for.

We shouldn't be so quick to ask, "How's that possible?" If the Scriptures, the Word from the Almighty, says, "the peace of God … will guard your hearts and your minds in Christ Jesus," maybe we should just accept that truth. After all, we don't have to understand how electricity travels through wires from its generation point to our light switches and from there to the lamps in our homes. We just flip the switch and trust that the lamps will illuminate. Our thirst for knowledge may be a good thing, but when it comes to the Word of God, we might try simply accepting God's instructions and obeying what the Lord says. To be truthful, we have but two options when it comes to the things God has told us: we either believe or we don't believe. If we choose not to believe, it shouldn't surprise us if our ways become muddled and fail.

God can and does make all things work together for the good of those who love God and are called according to His great purpose (Romans 8:28). When bad times assault our lives, it's hard to believe that, isn't it? We balk when pain and sorrow and loneliness come our way. How can it be that "in all things God works for the good" in the midst of our miserable times? Jesus came from heaven to earth to help us live the *divine life*, a life very different than the ordinary lives of others who have no relationship with God.

God wants that divine life for every one of His creatures.

He's not willing that any perish and fail to enter His kingdom, or His sphere of influence. He wants all of His sheep to be in His pasture.

Divine Life

What is the *divine life*? In 2 Peter 1:3, 4, the apostle said,

> His divine power has given us everything we need for life and godliness through our knowledge of him who called us by his own glory and goodness. Through these he has given us his very great and precious promises, so that through them you may participate in *the divine nature* and escape the corruption in the world caused by evil desires.

Peter said that, through God's very great and precious promises, we may participate in *the divine nature* (and escape the corruption in the world). "The divine nature"—what is that? Apparently, it's having the very nature of God Himself. Is that possible?

In the Matthew 6 prayer mentioned above, Jesus told us to pray, "... your kingdom come, your will be done on earth as it is in heaven" (Matthew 6:10). That prayer has been memorized widely and, as a result, has become a rote, mechanical quotation without much meaning to most people.

But what did Jesus mean? He taught us to pray that God's kingdom, or the Lord's territory of rule, control and influence, would actually *come to the earth*. Through the centuries, countless numbers of Christ-followers have experienced the rule of God on earth, because the kingdom comes to individuals within their spirits, not to nations or real estate.

But Jesus goes on to elaborate on the meaning of the request in His prayer. "Your will be done," He said, "on earth as it is in heaven." He is essentially saying that we should strive to bring God's heavenly environment and desires to *this* earth. The environment of God and His heaven (His native country) should be duplicated here and now in this physical universe. Of course, the physical world around us is corrupt and should be escaped from, according to Peter. But we should "participate" in the divine nature even while we are in this world.

For example: Does God want us to worry in heaven? Does God want us to be downcast in heaven? Does He want us to be in pain in heaven? Of course not. So, we should be about the business of replicating that condition on earth. But how do we create that kind of environment here and now?

That's the *divine life!* The key is "the Lord's territory of rule and control." If God is ruling over us internally and is in control of our lives, that's the atmosphere of heaven that will change everything for us. If we could only sense His presence and understand His control of all things in the universe, we could settle back and trust Him to care for us, to lead us and to heal us. Can you imagine living in heaven and in the presence of the God of all creation? As long as you can live in that presence, you will enjoy a divine life. No worries. No sorrows. No loneliness. Nothing negative at all. It's a state of faith.

If we could only remember, in good times and in bad times, no matter our circumstances, that we have a Savior in Jesus Christ, then our lives would be incredibly different and blessed. The presence of Christ would be palpable. But wait! Didn't we say that Jesus is in heaven, seated next to the Father's throne? Yes. And that is exactly why Holy Spirit was sent by Jesus to live IN US! The Spirit is, in fact, *the Spirit of Jesus.* If the Spirit is in us, then the essence of heaven is also in us.

Romans 8:9 tells us, "You, however, are controlled not by the sinful nature but by the Spirit, if the Spirit of God lives in you. And if anyone does not have the *Spirit of Christ*, he does not belong to Christ."

Did you notice that Holy Spirit is called both the "Spirit of God" and the "Spirit of Christ?" How's that possible? Because the Triune God is one God in three persons. There are no dividing lines. When Jesus left the earth, He asked God the Father to send Holy Spirit in Jesus' Name, to be with us and in us. So, bottom line, we have the Spirit of the Savior with us at all times. The gentle Jesus, the sacrificial Jesus, the conquering Jesus, the all-powerful Jesus is residing in us all the time. What an astonishing thing to consider! We can live the divine life, here and now! It will be an unconquerable life, the heavenly or divine life, even before we finally inherit eternal life in heaven.

The apostle Paul blessed the believers in Thessalonica with these words: "Now may the Lord of peace himself give you peace at all times and in every way. The Lord be with all of you" (2 Thessalonians 3:16). The apostle called Jesus "the Lord of peace." What did he mean by that? I believe Paul was telling us that Jesus is the GIVER of peace (He said, "Peace I leave with you; my peace I give you"). But Jesus is also the MAKER of peace (in Ephesians 2:14), we are told, "For he himself is our peace, who has made the two one and destroyed the barrier, the dividing wall of hostility...").

Jesus is the "One-maker," bringing together God and humanity, Jew and Gentile, heavenly beings and earthly beings. He brings peace to all things, everywhere—between nations and tribes, between individuals and churches. That's Christ's plan and work. It's bigger than we ever imagined. Because He is the peace GIVER and the peace MAKER. If that is true, what should be our priority as believers?

The presence of Jesus in our lives ought to bring peace, comfort and healing to us and to others. There may be other reasons for our pain—especially if it's physical pain. But even in the case of physical pain, many believers have experienced miraculous healing in their body. When my wife Laurette was near death from breast cancer, she never suffered pain. She endured lots of fatigue, but not pain. I tried to get her to take morphine pills, and she refused. She just slowly slipped away into the arms of Jesus, into His peace. I truly believe God gave her tremendous peace at the end, a foretaste of heaven. The presence of our Lord can often do miracles in our suffering and sorrow. He is, after all, the Prince of Peace.

Sometimes our enemy, Satan, tries to plant the idea that Jesus won't help us, doesn't bother with people like us, doesn't care about our hurts and sorrows. This is an emphatic lie. If we know anything at all about our Savior, we know that He desperately cares for us. He sees our every teardrop. And He says to us, "I understand. I suffered too. There's a new experience coming that you won't believe! So, be of good cheer. I've overcome the world, and you can too."

The Balm in Gilead

The prophet Jeremiah identified with his people and wrote, "Since my people are crushed, I am crushed; I mourn, and horror grips me. *Is there no balm in Gilead? Is there no physician there?* Why then is there no healing for the wound of my people?" (Jeremiah 8:21, 22).

A "balm" is a healing salve. Two hundred years ago or more, the enslaved people of America sang a song that answered Jeremiah's important question: "Is there no balm in Gilead?" As they labored in the cruel fields of plantations, those mistreated people courageously sang the *positive answer!*

> There is a balm in Gilead to make the wounded whole.

There is a balm in Gilead to heal the sin-sick soul.

Sometimes I feel discouraged, and think my work's in vain.

But then the Holy Spirit revives my soul again.

The balm or healing salve of Gilead is, of course, the great Triune God. God the Father has loved us from the very beginning of time, and His love will never end. With His life, Jesus God's Son, paid the ransom to take away our sins and sinful nature. And Holy Spirit comes to take up His residence in us, to empower us, to protect us, and to assure us of our eternal salvation. What a blessing to be loved by the Triune God! We are loved by the *whole* of God!

Sometimes we need to ask ourselves, "Do I really believe in a *supernatural* Jesus?" Yes, Jesus was a real man with flesh and blood. History attests to that. And His sacrifice for us in His human body was more painful than we can imagine. The Bible attests to that. But though He was a man, He was also *much more* than simply a man! He is the One who was dead yet is alive forever! He is the eternal God the Son. He is our Shalom, our peace. He was and is supernatural!

At times, when I'm nervous about something ominous, when my heart is overwhelmed with grief or fear or pain, I like to quote an old song we sang many years ago called "Peace, Perfect Peace." You may have heard it or sung it yourself. It was written by an Englishman named Edward Bickersteth in 1875. He was preceded in death by his wife of many years and some of his children. In other words, he was alone when he wrote this hymn. Bear that in mind as you read these wonderful, peaceful words: "Peace, perfect peace, in this dark world of sin: The blood of Jesus whispers *peace within*."

I often repeat that phrase several times, and it seems to settle my soul. For three more verses, Bickersteth continues to talk of "thronging duties pressed," and "sorrows surging round," and "loved ones far away," and "our future all unknown"—all the trials that come our way. He was familiar with them all; he had experienced them all. But then in the last verse Edward Bickersteth declares confidently: "It is enough; earth's struggles soon shall cease, And Jesus call us to heaven's perfect peace."

And He really does! He calls us to be with Him and enjoy heaven's perfect peace forever. Jesus Himself wants to be our Peace—peace in our mind, in our soul and especially in our heart or spirit. We may not think about it this way, but when we allow our heart to be overly concerned and burdened with the details of this life, about the great disappointments of our journey, we may be softly rejecting the Lord Jesus Who stands at the door of our heart and knocks, wanting to come in and comfort us with His peace.

We need the peace He offers us. I myself have felt that "peace that passes all understanding." When my wife Laurette died and I was in the depths of despair, I determined to thank the Lord for giving me such a wonderful partner for so many years. "O God, You are so kind and so good," I told Him. "You have blessed me beyond measure. Thank you so very, very much!" And that thankfulness eased my pain and covered me with peace.

I would have wished for many more years together with Laurette. But eventually, it seemed selfish of me to want more. Even if God did give me more time with her, I wonder if I would perhaps become bitter and resentful toward Him when she finally did go to be with Him. So, I tried to remind myself of how blessed I had been, and what a great gift God had given me, (not to mention the four children we had together) and I vowed to thank Him profusely forever. When my second wife also died, I was so used to thanking God, I just did the very same thing with regard to my second wife Patricia. I was profoundly thankful for God's consolation.

Relieving the Pain of Others

There's something else that's very important. In the depth of our wintertime, we can relieve our own stressed soul by reaching out to help someone else. When we write a note or call on the phone to a person who is experiencing grief, or loss, or any kind of pain, the very act of reaching beyond ourselves will unburden our own heart. Apparently, God created us in such a way that helping another person helps our own situation. So, keep that in mind when you are swamped with discouragement.

Jesus is the great physician. He wants us to be healthy and well. Why would we not want the great physician to come into our life and minister to us? Jeremiah asked, "Is there no physician there?" Today, we can affirm that, "Yes, there is the Great Physician, Jesus, who heals all our diseases and dispels our pain and sorrows." We dare not keep the door of our heart bolted.

Many of us say, "We trust in Jesus." That's easy to say in good times. But when times get very difficult, lonesome and painful, when we hurt badly, then our words take on special significance and meaning. We should trust Jesus in the worst of times, not just on sunny days. We must not be "fair weather Christians."

When we suffer loss, instead of dwelling on our personal pain, we should search for the things we've gained, the blessings we've enjoyed, and thank God and proclaim those victories for ourselves and others! Because of the sacrifice of our Lord, we have access to Father God, with Jesus as our advocate and lover of our soul. He purchased our freedom at an inconceivable cost—His own life on the cross. He is, in fact, OUR PEACE with God. He is our Shalom with the Divine.

Long ago, the prophet Isaiah wrote, "You [God] will keep in perfect peace him whose mind is steadfast, because he trusts in you" (Isaiah 26:3). Peace comes from God to all those whose minds are "steadfast, because he trusts in you [Holy God]." That's a promise from the Lord spoken more than 2700 years ago. And the promise has been renewed by God over and over again through the centuries. We don't have to worry that He has changed His mind.

We must have confidence in the goodness and loving intentions of God. His divine will is always our rescue, our redemption. He's like a craftsman who loves to restore old discarded furniture. He removes worn and chipped paint, carefully sands and smooths the surfaces, then applies a sparkling finish to the piece of furniture. That kind of care for us ought to fill us with thanksgiving. And thanksgiving is a huge part of healing.

Sometimes our heart needs to be convinced. So, I suggest we let our ears hear our mouth say it out loud: "I have peace with God through Jesus. My heart is at peace. My heart magnifies the Lord God. Thank you, Father, for the Shalom Peace you promised long ago to those who believe in you." When fears and sorrows rise, say, "I will not be afraid, and I will not be moved. I have peace within, because of my Savior Jesus."

Let your ears hear the declaration of your mouth.

5

Look Forward, Not Back

It's been said that there is a reason we were created with two eyes that both face forward in our head. I suppose the Lord could have created us with one eye in front and one in the back! But God knew we needed to always look forward and to focus our attention specifically on what's ahead. Why, then, do we so often try to look backward in our mind? I suppose it's natural. But that's the problem, isn't it? We are not called to be natural, but to be SUPER-natural people.

It's fine to occasionally look back to see where we've been, to learn lessons from the past. But we should *never live* in the past. We should always face the future. That's where God wants us to be. We are, in fact, *people of the future!* If we have faith in the supernatural God, we must live with Him in the "eternal now" that stretches far into the future.

I know of people who seem to perpetually live in the past—in some past hurt, some past offense, some past misfortune. But whether we're young or old, we can choose to *live forward.* Those who choose to look to the past usually have their future life shrivel before their eyes.

Children typically don't have a problem living forward, probably because they have very little of a past life. They're anxious to "get on with it;" they want to see what's next. But as we age, we build warehouses full of memories in our mind (often false or altered memories), and those flashes from the past may begin stealing our focus on the future. But even if we are in our 90s, there's always a future to look forward to. There's a new world that God has prepared for us, and we shall actually see it and experience it someday.

However, if we insist on looking back most of the time, we're unintentionally ending our life. A life without a future is a dead life. I suppose there are some people who deliberately intend on ending their life. But that certainly isn't what God has in mind. He has great and impactful plans for all who trust in Him.

So, we should live in anticipation, in excitement for what God is going to do in our life. It takes a certain amount of faith to live that way. Do we believe God is indeed moving us forward toward some blessed day? Then, don't spend too much time in the past.

One Thing I Do

The apostle Paul boldly said, "But one thing I do: Forgetting what is behind and straining toward what is ahead, I press on toward the goal to win the prize for which God has called me heavenward in Christ Jesus" (Philippians 3:13, 14). You and I are being called UPWARD, heavenward! We dare not turn back.

Did Paul have an easy life without pain and discouragement? If you've read the New Testament, you know his life was filled with untold trials and tribulations. How could he endure rejection and beatings and stoning and all sorts of dangers? Because he knew God had called him higher! His goal was to "win the prize" of God's calling. And it's the same for you and me. We too have been called higher. We probably have far fewer challenges than did the apostle Paul. So, we face fewer barriers to our goal. The problem is, we *lose sight* of the goal, and we turn our attention to the mundane negative details of this present life.

In *Letters to Children*, C. S. Lewis wrote, "Anyone in our world who devotes his whole life to seeking heaven will be like [Reepicheep, in *The Voyage of the Dawn Treader*]." I hope you've read Lewis's seven little books that comprise *The Chronicles of Narnia*. They were meant to be children's books, but adults like myself have become engrossed in the stories and we've been inspired by the lessons they illustrate. The books are very spiritual, even though they are about four English school children that enter a fantasy realm called Narnia.

One of Lewis's characters in *The Voyage of the Dawn Treader* is named "Reepicheep," and he is a three-foot tall mouse. In Narnia, many animals, as well as people, can talk. The talking mouse, Reepicheep, is a very noble, brave, and chivalrous little creature. Why did Lewis imagine a mouse to be a major character in his stories? Perhaps, like Reepicheep, we tend to see ourselves as small and insignificant in this world. But this mouse, though small, is very courageous and principled, and he's willing to take on any challenge for a noble cause: he's an example for you and me.

Near the end of *The Voyage of the Dawn Treader*, the mouse leaves the other characters behind, because he is finally where he always wanted to be—Aslan's country (or heaven). Aslan, if you didn't know, is a great lion who is the Christ figure in Lewis's stories. Lewis writes,

> No one in that boat doubted that they were seeing beyond the End of the World into Aslan's country. At that moment, with a crunch, the boat ran aground. The water was too shallow now for it. 'This,' said Reepicheep, 'is where I go on alone.' They did not even try to stop him, for everything now felt as if it had been fated or had happened before. They helped him lower his little coracle [smaller boat]. Then he took off his

sword ('I shall need it no more,' he said) and flung it far away across the lilied sea. Where it fell it stood upright with the hilt above the surface. Then he bade them good-bye, trying to be sad for their sakes; but he was quivering with happiness. Lucy, for the first and last time, did what she had always wanted to do, taking him in her arms and caressing him. Then hastily he got into his coracle and took his paddle, and the current caught it and away he went, very black against the lilies. But no lilies grew on the wave; it was a smooth green slope. The coracle went more and more quickly, and beautifully it rushed up the wave's side. For one split second they saw its shape and Reepicheep's on the very top. Then it vanished, and since that moment no one can truly claim to have seen Reepicheep the Mouse. But my belief is that he came safe to Aslan's country and is alive there to this day.

In the stories of *The Chronicles of Narnia*, we find Reepicheep running up the hills and mountains ahead of the others and yelling, "onward and upward!" He's leading the way—just a little mouse! We too ought to be running ahead of our family, friends, and church members urging them "onward and upward," looking ahead and never hanging our head in despair.

Like Lewis's little mouse, children don't have to be told to look forward. No matter how many times we entertain them, they excitedly say, "Yay, that's fun. What's next?" They naturally think about what's ahead. Even if they know what's coming and have seen it dozens of times, they say, "Do it again!" And again … and again!

The Future Forward

There's always some kind of future in front of us, even if

we are in our 90s. A new world awaits us, a world in which we'll never grow old. Excitement rises as we look forward to God's working in our life. This forward-looking attitude helps us recover from painful events and haunting memories. We must have faith that God is moving us forward toward some bright tomorrow.

I have wonderful memories of Laurette, the wife of my youth. And I also have warm memories of Patricia, the wife of my later years, my consolation. Sometimes I bask in those thoughts and picture us in happy and exciting times. But I've learned to not linger there too long. To live in memory for extended periods of time is to spiral down into depression. So, when I remember those times, I just say, "Thank you, Lord, for the gift of those wonderful times. You've been so, so good to me. My, how you have blessed me!" Even in the midst of suffering, it's still possible to consider how God has given us multitudes of good gifts—so many enjoyable days. We simply cannot allow our present suffering to steal the memories of blessed times.

There's usually a sense of excitement in the days of our youth. The young look forward and expect something new to happen. They can't wait for the next great adventure. But when we grow older, our memories can entrap us into melancholy or periods of regret. We long for some past happiness, but it's impossible to go backward. That situation may produce sadness or destructive longings. We wish for another time, a time that is no more, and never can be again. But if we allow ourselves to go to that moment in the past, we can become forlorn, we can rob ourselves of the new thing that will bring us joy.

If we too often look backward, we may sometimes *miss what's ahead*. Our enemy Satan tries to convince us that there's nothing in the future for us, and we end up thinking only of the "good ol' days." But listen, there is ALWAYS something ahead! It's the "now" that we possess, a "now" that's always moving forward. We can't relive the past or change it in any way. But we can treasure the now. Don't let the present slip through your fingers.

Even when our dreams seem dead and gone, God is able to instill us with new dreams and new visions for tomorrow. I think it's important to ask the Lord how we may serve Him and how we may serve others. Adventure lies in *unselfish service*. If we try to serve only ourselves we'll fail. Satisfaction comes as a byproduct of serving others. Perhaps we won't recapture some particular enjoyable time in our life, but God will give us expansive and exciting new plans for the future. That is, if we don't give up on life. Life is a precious thing, and it's a gift from the God of all Creation. We must not squander it, misuse it, and fail to appreciate it.

Jesus Himself always looked forward. He is "the God Who came near," as Max Lucado said. And Jesus came to identify with the poor and the hurting, to become a "nobody" like the rest of us. God is not aloof. He weeps with us and hurts with us. One day He will make everything right. If that is His priority and His focus, we should have that same priority and focus. For, we are His people, His means of accomplishing His will.

Submit to God

It's imperative that we submit or surrender to God's will. I know most of us understand that truth. But do we also submit to His *timing*? The Lord may not instantly give us exactly what we desire. But He will give us what we *need* in due time, and He'll give us our desires in *His own* timing. I know of people who believe their life is over, and they are ready to go and be with the Lord—right now. But the choice and the timing of our home-going is not up to us. We're not our own. The timing of our departure belongs to God alone. When God says, "Your life is over," *then* it's over. And not one second before. Not one second later. In addition to God's will, we also must submit to His perfect timing. How often does Scripture tell us, "In the fullness of time …"? Everything God does, He does on time, and in *His time!*

In the depths of our pain, we should strain forward and look ahead to "springtime." But springtime only comes for those who have the faith to see it. The things I'm talking about are not natural phenomena; they are seen by faith. Faith itself is a supernatural exercise. It takes the power of the holy God to embrace faith. Because faith doesn't depend on the "reality" that we can see. It's not evident to our senses. We must be aware of a higher reality, a truer true. Yes, we can know what this existence makes plain. But there is more. Much more.

Real springtime can only be seen with spiritual eyes— through faith. And true springtime always points us and moves us forward *toward* our creator. Satan, evil personified, is intent on pulling us backward, convincing us to "be reasonable," and "just look around at the way the world works." The Evil One reminds us of our failures and tries to make us believe that the future will be just like the past, including a repetition of past sins and embarrassing mistakes. We can count on this: the Evil One is a liar and wants to destroy every believer in Christ, including you and me. The devil is the spoiler who is against our Lord. And he is responsible for the destruction of billions of people who might otherwise believe and be saved.

When you think about it, memory is both a blessing and a curse. It all depends on you and me. It's a blessing that we use to remember all that God has done for us. As I scan my life, I realize that, even as a child, God was with me and comforted me in the dark days of World War II. So many instances come to mind as I think of how God was with me and kept me from doing stupid things or saved me from dangerous times. The Lord reminds me of His great love for the little "me."

But memory can also be a curse, as the devil uses it to remind me of my many failures. If he's doing that to you, send him packing by declaring that God is *for you, not against you.* God loves you and always will. Don't let the devil have the last word. Believe what God says and realize that Satan is a liar who wants you to be lost ... like he is.

It's always a strong temptation to not only remember your failures, but also to *live in them.* I urge you to *break free!* You can be free of the devil's grip by praising God the Father (the devil hates that!) and by quoting Scriptures to the Evil One in the midst of his attacks on you. The ancient Scriptures are a strong defense against satanic attacks. That's the strategy that Jesus used when He was tempted by Satan in the desert as He began His ministry.

It Is Written

I believe the passage in Matthew 4 was recorded specifically for you and me, so we would have a strategy for success against our enemy. In the passage in Matthew 4, Jesus responded with a Scripture to each challenge or temptation from Satan. The Lord said, "It is written: 'Man does not live on bread alone, but on every word that comes from the mouth of God.'" Then He said, "It is also written: 'Do not put the Lord your God to the test.'" And finally, He answered, "Away from me, Satan! For it is written: 'Worship the Lord your God and serve Him only.'"

Think of that strategy! Jesus first pointed out that our physical needs are not as important as our spiritual needs. We need "every word that comes from the mouth of God." Then Jesus affirmed that we must not "put the Lord our God to the test" by calling on Him to convince either ourselves or others of God's miraculous care for us. And finally, Jesus threw the Truth in Satan's teeth by saying, "worship the Lord your God, and serve Him only." Yes, whether Satan acknowledges it or not, God is "your (the devil's) God also"—that is, God is supreme and exalted above Satan, and every knee will bow someday, including Satan's. The devil will be cast away from "his God." There is no other God. What an amazing strategy for success against the Evil One!

The daughter of a Wesleyan Methodist pastor, Helen Lemmel was born in Wardle, England in 1864. She came to America in the early 1900s and enjoyed a successful career in music and teaching. She wrote more than 500 hymns, in addition to her children's books. She taught at Moody Bible Institute and BIOLA in Los Angeles. In 1922, Helen wrote a hymn that describes the spirit we should have:

> Turn your eyes upon Jesus,
>
> Look full in His wonderful face,
>
> And the things of earth will grow strangely dim
>
> In the light of His glory and grace.

When we "turn our eyes upon Jesus," we turn toward the future. For He is the God of today and, especially, the God of tomorrow. We look forward to living with Him forever.

I've already mentioned the Hebrew word, *Aliyah*. It colorfully describes our journey toward God. And it generally means "going up" or "ascending." Today, emigrants that travel to Israel say, "I'm making Aliyah." The "Songs of Ascent" could also be called, "Songs of Aliyah." Those wonderful psalms were the ones God's people sang as they climbed the hills to Jerusalem as they entered the Temple. And we too are "making Aliyah." We're going up to the heavenly Zion, the beautiful city of God.

Like C. S. Lewis's noble little mouse, Reepicheep, we should be running up hills and mountains shouting, "onward and upward!" The courageous little mouse was always searching for Aslan's (Christ's) country (heaven). And that should be our preoccupation—our passion!—as well. We can actually experience heaven here and now by looking forward, not back, having heaven in the forefront of our mind and heart, living with that heavenly mindset. Use the "eyes" in the "front of your head."

So, I strongly urge you to look ahead and look up toward heaven. *Live forward* rather than backward.

Turn your eyes upon Jesus and look full in His wonderful face!

6

Get Over and Out of Yourself

Rick Warren, in his runaway bestseller, *The Purpose Driven Life*, begins his book with these startling words:

It's not about you.

The purpose of your life is far greater than your own personal fulfillment, your peace of mind, or even your happiness. It's far greater than your family, your career, or even your wildest dreams and ambitions. If you want to know why you were placed on this planet, you must begin with God. You were born *by* his purpose and *for* his purpose.

Warren is absolutely right, and his blockbuster book sold millions, because most people know, down deep, that our lives need purpose. And most people have discovered that self-centered purpose doesn't satisfy.

Many of us struggle with the meaning of life in general and in our own lives specifically. It plagues us and haunts us. Viktor Frankl wrote a book called, *Man's Search for Meaning*, and for many people, that's exactly what they're looking for: something that makes sense of their life. Interestingly, that "making sense of their life" cannot be found in money or security, in fame or notoriety, in athletic ability, even in a wonderful life partner—or anything else. Some make fun of that truth and say, "Well, I'd like to have a lot of money and fame and a beautiful life partner, because I'll bet I could find happiness!"

But time and again, that has been proved false. Very successful people have confessed openly that their lives are miserable because of all those coveted things. But many of us just won't listen.

God has created us so that the more we focus on ourselves, the less satisfied we are with life. But the reverse is also true: the more we focus on improving the lives of other people, the more satisfied we become. I'm sure there are multitudes that would disagree, but that's what I have seen over and over in my long life. *We seem to be created for community and appreciation for others.* I can't really explain it. But it's simply my observation from many years of living in a variety of situations, being around both wealth and poverty. I've known wealthy people who were terribly unhappy, and I've known poor people who were very happy. But then, I've known wealthy people who have learned the secret of generosity—and have ended up happy!

Many commentators have noticed that *happiness* is a *by-product* of reaching beyond self. In Philippians 2:3, 4, for example, the apostle Paul says, "Do nothing out of selfish ambition or vain conceit, but in humility consider others better than yourselves. Each of you should look not only to your own interests, but also to the interests of others." Now, that's the way to live!

Here's what I've seen. Those who are self-focused, especially if they are lost in their own misery, don't get better. They may even get worse. They are perpetually stuck in a slime-covered pit from which it's impossible to escape. Perhaps, the Lord made it that way—in order to escape the pit, we must look to others to get help and give help. Love is the rope that's let down into our prison to lift us up.

I'm very concerned for those who have allowed past failures, or circumstances, or pain to get them down. Perhaps, it's because I've been down—many times. And I know the dismal feelings at the bottom. I want to find a way to extricate those in that pit.

Many people experience *loneliness*. They feel detached and isolated. That's an awful situation. Loneliness can be a problem, even in churches where there are crowds of people, because though there are plenty of others around, some of us just don't feel connected to any one person. I only know of one solution to that problem: we must *aggressively* reach out to others. Force them to speak to you if you are lonely, because they too may be in a self-isolated cocoon. I know it's uncomfortable, but someone has to make the first move. We can't sit back and wait for others to shake our hand or wish us well or just say hello. Families and churches alike are important to God. Psalm 68:6 says, the Lord "sets the lonely in families."

Sometimes isolation is almost an intentional thing, or at least it may be understandable. People tend to avoid hurting people or unhappy people, not necessarily because they don't care, but because they don't know what to say or how to help. And since all of us have our own problems, it's easy to just choose alienation, rather than community. However, I have come to believe that only community can alleviate the problem of loneliness.

In his book, *A Grace Disguised*, Jerry Sittser writes, "Loss leads to a confusion of identity." So, whether it's illness, death, divorce, abandonment, or anything else, aloneness puts us into a tailspin of doubt concerning our identity. If we lose sight of our true identity as believers, God can give us a new identity. He restores and recreates if we will cooperate with Him by faith. When any of these challenges come our way, we should dig deep into that true identity that God alone grants us, which is, "I am a child of the living God!"

As I've repeatedly emphasized, we're satisfied only when

we are reaching beyond ourselves, when we're *serving* others. When we buy a nice gift for ourselves, we're pleased only briefly. Then the pleasure quickly wears off. The "nice gift" is new for only a short time, then turns to commonplace or revulsion. On the other hand, when we give a thoughtful gift to someone else, especially if it costs us some sacrifice, we're filled with wonderful, happy feelings and that sense continues with warm memories. Maybe that's why, in Paul's final address to the Ephesian elders, he quoted Jesus, saying, "It is more blessed to give than to receive" (Acts 20:35). I've heard a lot of people make jokes about that statement by Jesus, probably because it sounds so ridiculous. But what if Jesus was giving us a very serious, but simple secret or formula for blessedness? Many of us may have missed out on true happiness.

I can remember a time when I was able to give a substantial monetary gift (substantial at least to me!) to a ministry that drills water wells in isolated villages across the world. The wells result in saving lives, especially the lives of vulnerable children, many of whom die from contaminated water. That gift lingers in my memory and warms my soul. I've gotten far more joy from that moment of giving than from any gift I've ever received for myself.

Giving Gifts

So, my greatest joys have been times when I was able to give an extravagant gift to someone else. We must "get over ourselves"—and discover that we are not the center of the universe. We should think of others, rather than our own joys or even our pain and suffering. Often, our own pain and discouragement can confine our attention to ourselves. But as Rick Warren says, "It's not about you." It's all about God. Intense attention toward oneself is actually the cause of terrible feelings of sadness, depression, and loneliness.

I heard a story of one of the richest men in American history who became gravely ill. Doctors could do nothing for him. His system could tolerate no food. Finally, the man, who could afford the costliest food, was able to eat only bread and water. As he began to get his affairs in order and prepare to die, he also began giving away his incredible wealth, and to his great surprise, he became whole and healthy again.

Even spiritual gifts are not to be used selfishly or hoarded. Jesus said, "Heal the sick, raise the dead, cleanse those who have leprosy, drive out demons. Freely you have received, freely give" (Matthew 10:8). As we mentioned in the last chapter, both our eyes face forward. We should be looking around to see whom we may bless. We need to get *over* ourselves. But we also need to get *out* of ourselves. Many of us pity ourselves—"Poor me, I hurt so bad, I'm so stressed and broken." Yes, we hurt. We all hurt because that's the nature of this fallen world. But many people around us are in worse shape than we are. We need to encourage ourselves, and we need to get out of ourselves.

Much of our conflict and disillusionment in life stems from our failure to remember what God has done for us. We have a tendency to be complainers, self-absorbed whiners. It's a very dangerous place to be, because it's where the children of Israel were in the days of the rebellion in the Sinai desert. They complained about everything.

Even after God had miraculously delivered them from Egyptian bondage through the Red Sea, they accused Him of leading them into the desert to abandon them to starvation. "We have no water!" "We have no food!" "We hate this bread you're giving us!" "We want meat!" Had they learned nothing? But sometimes you and I may be no different. We quickly forget the times of blessings, the times of deliverance we've had from the Lord. It's sort of a constant refrain, "What have you done for me lately, God?" While we're complaining about our pain or our loss, we tend to lose sight of and miss out on the blessings the Lord is providing.

James said, "Draw near to God and He will draw near to you" (James 4:8). God will not force Himself on anyone. He offers us Himself, but relationship is up to us. We can draw near to the Lord by acknowledging that most of our life has been good and blessed, and by not railing against Him because of the "lean times" or the present suffering we may be experiencing.

For my part, the pain and loss in my own life have resulted in me a ravenous hunger for heaven and a strong desire to ease the pain of others. I credit most of that hunger with the coming of Holy Spirit into my life. I suppose He was always in my life to some degree, but in my latter days, the Spirit has come with an amazing force and caused me to hunger for more of the Father, more of the Son, and more of the Spirit.

David, the great shepherd king of Israel, said, "Why are you downcast, O my soul? Why so disturbed within me? Put your hope in God, for I will yet praise him, my Savior and my God. My soul is downcast within me; therefore I will remember you from the land of Jordan, the heights of Hermon—from Mount Mizar" (Psalm 42:5, 6).

There's amazing wisdom in David's musings. He talked to himself and said, "Why are downcast, O my soul? Why so disturbed within me?" That's the kind of "self-talking-to" that we should consider doing when we're feeling low! Talk to yourself and say, "Put your hope in God!" And then praise God! He's worthy and that praise can actually heal us! David continued by saying that his soul was downcast within him, so *he will remember the Lord.* Now, there's a suggestion that can pull us up out of the pit: Remember the Lord!

By refocusing our attention from our troubles to the Maker of all things, we'll encourage our "downcast soul." We will *get out of ourselves*. And when you think about it, to get out of ourselves is to get out of the "valley of despair." We should seriously consider reaching out to others, for our good, but mostly for *their* good. When we do that, *we are most like God*, who always thinks about others and desires to help others.

How to Escape the Pit

How do we "get out of ourselves?" Well, we do that by understanding that it's not about us. We are not "self-made" people. The Lord has given us everything we have, our riches (such as they are) and our talents and abilities. We owe everything, not only to God who created us, but also to those who loved us and molded and shaped us and gave us birth. We owe it all to those who will be with us at our final breath. This is very humbling. Without humility, God cannot use us or bless us. But don't worry; if you can't seem to humble yourself, God will do it for you!

It's a delicate balance. We must arm ourselves with a "good self-image." But at the same time, we also must not think too highly of ourselves. For as Christ-followers, we must have an honest view of self. In and of ourselves, we're not that impressive. All of us have become like one who is unclean, the Bible says, and our righteous acts are as "filthy rags" (Isaiah 64:6). That means no one has a right to boast. We are not "good people," because we all sin and fall short of God's high hope for us.

On the other hand, we are God's beloved ones. In that well-known passage, John 3:16, it says, "God so loved the world that he gave his one and only Son, that whoever believes in him shall not perish but have eternal life." When it says, "God so loved the world," that means all humans, including you and me. *You are God's beloved*; so beloved that God gave His one and only Son for your salvation. That truth gives us inestimable worth. So, the thing that gives us worth is God's valuation of us. It's indeed a delicate balance between thinking too highly of ourselves and thinking too little of ourselves. The key is to think of ourselves, if at all, in the way God sees us. Because, "It's not about us; it's all about God."

In a word, selfishness is very *destructive*. It tends to build a prison all around us. I've known people who could think of nothing but their own wellbeing. "What does this do for me? What will I gain from this?" they wonder. If they think of others at all, it's merely how others relate to them. There are people who never get a glimpse of the truth that *giving to others* is a way to bless oneself. As I've tried to say, the Creator seems to have built into our psyche the concept that we must think of and work toward the good of others, or the community, in order to be genuinely happy. And not to concentrate only on our own good.

I ought to note that it's also true that if we don't appreciate ourselves as a creation of God, we won't appreciate other people and want to bless them. I've found it very effective to pray and ask God to help me see people as He sees them. I learned of someone, years ago, who prayed, "Lord, may my heart be broken by the things that break Your Heart." What a remarkable prayer! If a significant number of us joined in that kind of prayer, it would truly revolutionize our world!

When I say, "Get Over and Out of Yourself," I certainly do not mean that we should never think of our own life. That would be nearly impossible. Because of a God-given instinct, we have an innate drive to preserve ourselves and treat ourselves well. I'm simply saying that we must fight against an inordinate amount of concern for our own life and affairs. Thinking too much about us steals our attention away from others.

If we can think of nothing but our own problems and misery, we're blinded to the blessings God is still giving us, and we're blinded to the needs of others, which may be greater than our own needs. So, we should open our eyes to the world of others. I've become nearly overwhelmed by the critical needs of the multitudes around me, the need for relieving their pain and desperation and, especially, the need for them to embrace the gospel of Jesus. So many people are facing their world all alone, with no one to comfort them and lift them up.

I truly believe God is doing something amazing in our lives, in our day! However, that "something" is, for the most part, *hidden*. I remember the story of Joseph in Genesis chapters 37 to 50. His life was one of risk and reward. If we want to enjoy the rewards of free will, we must be willing to risk. Joseph, the son of Jacob, lived an extraordinary life of faith, risking it all to follow the leading of God. The purpose in his life's journey was mostly hidden, only revealed step-by-step by the Lord. It's worth reading again.

The hidden blessings of Joseph's life were manifest when he was older, only after many difficult trials. As he revealed himself in his exalted position in Egypt, his brothers were stunned and afraid. Joseph finally understood that God was using him and all circumstances of his life for a hidden, higher good. Joseph told the brothers, "I am your brother Joseph, the one you sold into Egypt! And now, do not be distressed, and do not be angry with yourselves for selling me here, because it was to save lives that God sent me ahead of you" (Genesis 45:4, 5). Joseph was instrumental in saving Egypt, his family, and the whole Mediterranean world. God's will and work is often hidden, even to you and me!

Protecting Others

Perhaps it's because of the fatherly instincts I've developed as I've grown older, but I feel the need to protect the vulnerable people among us—perhaps those who have so little in material goods, those who are being enslaved, those who have no hope in this life. But there's another kind of protection that we usually don't think about. There are things that I know that are dark secrets of the people I love. *Those secrets must be kept hidden.* Why? Because their revelation will bring shame and embarrassment to people I love. Usually, they have overcome those hidden things, and it's up to me to keep them hidden.

But shouldn't everything come to light? No, not everything. That, in fact, is Satan's way of doing things. He's interested in exposing weaknesses and sins. He's the great accuser of the brothers and sisters in Christ. Just when we've finally overcome our shameful past, Satan (sometimes in the form of other people) comes along to accuse us again and cause us to remember our dark past. Everyone, and I mean everyone, has things of which they are not proud. God tells us that He has deliberately *forgotten our shortcomings,* but the enemy of our soul loves to expose them again and again.

So, you and I should try our best to forget dark things in the past, something like the way God forgives and "forgets." We don't want to be found doing the work of Satan, bringing up old shortcomings and sins and throwing them back at our loved ones, or even diminishing our enemies, for that matter. I've found that we have a tendency to bring up dark things in an attempt to make a joke, or to make light of someone, or to make ourselves look better, even exposing someone we love. There's an evil urge in our heart to make ourselves look good and "take others down a notch." That must not be true of us.

James said, "Whoever turns a sinner from the error of his way will save him from death and cover over a multitude of sins" (James 5:20). We ought to be in the business of "covering over a multitude of sins" of both our loved ones and our enemies, because that's God's great desire. Jesus came to save us from our sins. Let's not bring them back up in order to get a laugh or make ourselves look good. Protect the reputation of *everyone*. Allow God to be the only judge of humanity.

I think "getting out of yourself" is actually *a great escape* from the "prison of self." When we think more about blessing others than we think about protecting our own public image, we're walking free of the confinement into which the devil has led us. Paul tells us, "It is for freedom that Christ has set us free" (Galatians 5:1). The apostle was thinking of the Mosaic law and any other law that constrains us. But we can also think of that freedom as breaking free from our own internal laws or compulsions, as well. Sometimes we're enslaved by our own inner demands. I would suggest that we break free of the slavery of self-interest. That's what "getting out of yourself" is all about.

I'm concerned for all those who are facing life alone, either because they have chosen to be alone, or because they are abandoned, or because a loved one has died. They are severely suffering with all kinds of pain. And I wonder how to help them. I certainly don't have all the answers, but through my own suffering, I've discovered a few of the answers.

Getting Out of Self

As we conclude this chapter, we ask: How can we relieve the pain and discouragement of our lives and the lives of others? There's no doubt that God is the only real solution. Of course, one way is to anesthetize ourselves, with some sort of drug or alcohol. Many millions of people are doing that at this very moment. But that's not the good way. That way only pushes the solution farther into the future, and probably damages the present. A deeper and better answer is to *get over and out of yourself.* People who are plagued with illnesses or great loss have found that, by refocusing their attention on others rather than themselves, they can bless others and, at the same time, encourage themselves and diminish their own pain and loss. Our individual lives are very overrated. Our lives *together* IN CHRIST is the real solution.

The apostle Paul tells us:

> But because of his great love for us, God, who is rich in mercy, made us alive with Christ even when we were dead in transgressions—it is by grace you have been saved. And God raised us up with Christ and seated us with him in the heavenly realms in Christ Jesus, in order that in the coming ages he might show the incomparable riches of his grace, expressed in his kindness to us in Christ Jesus (Ephesians 2:4-7).

What an astounding passage! It's filled with encouragement if we can only believe it and let it transform our lives. The key to this amazing scripture is *IN CHRIST.* We were made alive *with Christ.* God raised us up *with Christ.* He expressed His kindness *in Christ.* This passage elevates Jesus to the highest place under the Father. Can we embrace these truths? Can we allow them to speak comfort into our lives?

Keith and Kristyn Getty wrote a powerful worship song a few years ago, and Natalie Grant made a popular recording of it. Meditate on the uplifting words of "In Christ Alone," and let its inspiring thoughts minister peace to you in your weakness and despair:

> In Christ alone my hope is found
> He is my light, my strength, my song
> This Cornerstone, this solid ground

Firm through the fiercest drought and storm
What heights of love, what depths of peace
When fears are stilled, when strivings cease
My Comforter, my All in All
Here in the love of Christ I stand

Christ is the way to get over and out of ourselves. When He is the object of our lives, everything else will fade or fall into place. May the message of "In Christ Alone" help to free you from the prison of self.

7

There Is More

There is more is the title of a book by Brian Houston of Hillsong Church in Sydney, Australia. The subtitle is "When the World Says You Can't, God Says You Can." I love the whole idea behind the title and the book, and it's very much in line with the thinking and preaching of the marvelous author. Brian Houston is perhaps the most positive person I've ever listened to. His messages are always filled with hope and inspiration, as he admonishes his listeners that "the best is yet to be."

His book, according to Houston himself, was motivated by an expansive and exciting passage in Ephesians 3:20, that says, "Now to him who is able to do immeasurably more than we ask or imagine, according to his power that is at work within us, to him be glory in the church and in Christ Jesus throughout all generations, for ever and ever! Amen." Meditating on that scripture should fill every believer with profound trust in the power and goodness of God.

There is more is Houston's declaration or proclamation of confidence in the future, of God's power and plans for us, and of the watch care of God Almighty. It's also a battle cry *against* the apathy and defeatism that infects so much of our world and, often, the church! It seems there are people who only get excited when they are talking about doom and gloom. We all need more of Brian's kind of optimism and faith as we live our lives, and that's especially true for those who suffer with pain, guilt, loneliness, and discouragement.

"There is more" isn't some kind of resentful or stubborn statement. You may remember the 1936 movie classic, *Gone with the Wind*, starring Vivien Leigh and Clark Gable. The famous final line of the movie was from the character Scarlett O'Hara, played by Leigh. "Tomorrow is another day," Scarlett defiantly vowed. She was thinking of the great task of rebuilding Tara, her home and plantation. That's a type of resignation, or perhaps a sort of willfulness, an "in-your-face" kind of attitude.

Brian Houston's message, on the other hand, is a statement of steadfast faith in the power, goodness and faithfulness of God. He invites his readers and his listeners to "live with expectancy." And it's something that Christ-believers who are suffering attacks of pain and discouragement should carefully consider—and embrace. Like Houston, believers under attack should "dream big, and trust God." With a positive and empowering message by Houston, God has built Hillsong Church in Australia into a multi-campus church, with many locations around the world, under the leadership of Brian and his wife Bobbie. It's astounding what God can do through people that "get it!"

Some of us slip into depression as we feel our life is over, when we don't seem to have anything to live for or believe in, when our faith begins to waver. Pain, guilt, and bitterness can cause that feeling. But I want to remind you that a *feeling* is not necessarily a *truth*; it's simply a "feeling"—an emotional response that we can pay attention to or ignore. We must learn to differentiate between our feelings and the solid truth of a situation or condition. Just because we're lonely doesn't mean we'll be lonely for the rest of our days. Feelings, even negative ones, usually pass. We sleep and we wake up—and God renews our spirit. A new day dawns, and we have a new resolve to press on.

But there's a danger that we'll be diminished by our suffering. God doesn't want that to happen. We may end up defining ourselves by our current status. We tend to identify ourselves as "single," "alone," "ill" or "cancer victim," "the one who was abused or raped." But that's NOT who we truly are. That may be what has happened to us, but we're more than that. We're something far more valuable. We can be victimized by our own mind if we listen to the accusations of Satan. He's the one that continues to label us, far beyond the things that have happened to us. But we can label ourselves! We can declare ourselves as the "highly favored of God!"

We should always remember that our Creator wants to be FIRST in our life. He will not take a place behind loved ones, friends, hobbies, service to community, even ourselves. If we understand God's exalted person and position (He is the beginning and the end of all things!), we'll realize that He will not take a back seat to anyone or anything. The Lord is Supreme. And yet, He has a great future in store for those who earnestly love Him.

Turn to Life

I urge you to turn to life and *believe* (not feel) that *there is more*—more life, more love to share, more work to be done for the Lord. We simply *must not* allow feelings to dictate our behavior. My brother is a psychological therapist, and he likes to say, "It's easier to act your way into a new feeling, than to feel your way into a new way of acting." I believe he's absolutely right. Feelings are not solid ground for making decisions in life. As we begin to change the way we act, our feeling will certainly follow suit.

If we believe the future is hopeless or will always be the

same, we've become a "practical atheist." We may not intend to be an atheist, but we're behaving as one, because we've lost view of an extremely important truth: Jesus said, "With man this is impossible, but with God *all things* are possible" (Matthew 19:26). What's possible with God? ALL THINGS! What does "all" mean? It means ALL! We have no excuse to declare that "all is lost" when all things are possible with God. As long as there's breath, there's hope. In fact, for the Christ-follower, there is hope even *when breath ceases.* Even as we close our eyes for the last time, there is more! Heaven is about to break in upon us!

As long as there is a God in heaven and there is a Messiah at His right hand (and a Holy Spirit that lives right here in us), *there is more!* How can we lose hope while there's a Nick Vujicic in this world? Nick is a young man, born and raised in Australia, who has a rare disorder called tetra-amelia syndrome. Because of that disease, he was born with no arms or legs. And yet, today he's an inspiring evangelist and motivational speaker who travels the world, drawing great crowds to hear his messages of hope and courage. Somehow (I don't know how!), Nick can swim, surf, skateboard and get on with his life, *even without arms and legs.* He's married now, with a lovely wife. Listeners who claimed they were "hopeless," go away with a new sense of resolve and faith. And they're also a little ashamed of their complaints when they're blessed with all their limbs and faculties. Nick is an unbelievable gift to the world. His messages of optimism and faith have lifted thousands of downcast hearts. And Nick Vujicic would certainly say, "My friends, there is more! Much more!"

As long as there is a God, there is more. Because God's resources are limitless, and His willingness to reach out to us is ever present. By no means is He under obligation to meet our timetable. In His unfathomable wisdom, He accomplishes things in His time. He's not a "genie" to whom we can bark commands and have Him obey our every wish. God is sovereign, and He is eternal. That means He has all the time in the world. And He has all the blessings in the universe to do as He pleases. He also reminds us time and again that He loves us with an everlasting and extravagant love. And since He is eternal, *there is always more!*

Hope and a Future

We may not know God's immediate plans, but we do know how He feels about His people and what His intentions are toward us: "'I know the plans I have for you,' declares the LORD, 'plans to prosper you and not to harm you, plans to give you hope and a future'" (Jeremiah 29:11). Maybe one reason we allow ourselves to get dejected is that we're not sure God is *really* for us, or if He even cares about our situations.

We cry out in the middle of the night, but He doesn't seem to take notice or understand our pain. Long ago, the prophet Isaiah assured us, "The Sovereign Lord will wipe away the tears from all faces; he will remove the disgrace of his people from all the earth" (Isaiah 25:8). John renewed that promise in the New Testament in Revelation 21:4, "He will wipe every tear from their eyes. There will be no more death or mourning or crying or pain, for the old order of things has passed away." That's a promise for God's people—for those who trust Him and love Him.

What ugly thoughts sneak into our minds when we are weary or discouraged!—the very idea that God doesn't care about us! Peter told us, "Cast all your anxiety on him because he cares for you" (1 Peter 5:7). As one greeting card company began saying in 1944, "When you care enough to send the very best ..." [send our card]. God sent His very best, His own dear Son, for you and me and all the lonely, hurting people of the world. Yes, God cares very much for us; He records every tear we cry. And "He cared enough to send the very best."

What an exciting life we can live if we put our faith in God! Every step is a risk of sorts, but it's also a movement into the perfect will of God, with the possibility of great blessing. It has become something of a cliché, but nevertheless, it's still true that "We don't know what the future holds, but we know Who holds the future."

I've been thinking lately of our life of faith as *The Great Adventure*. We never know what's over the next hill or around the next corner. So, we live expectantly. God leads us up a high mountain, toward "His own native country," as C. S. Lewis used to call heaven. There are many dangers involved in our journey, but also tremendous opportunities for breathtaking vistas we've never seen before, places to rest and consider the adventure, as well as our ultimate goal.

We'll never enjoy the journey and the inspiring views unless we put one foot in front of the other. So, keep climbing. Upward we go, always upward, toward our heavenly Father—where there is astoundingly *more!* Finally, when we reach the end of our adventure at the top of the mountain, there's a door in the sky. And Jesus invites us to step through the door. There, just inside the doorway, waiting to embrace us is Jesus our Savior, and the Father and Creator of all things. As we step through the door in the sky, someone steps aside and we thankfully acknowledge that Holy Spirit has been our guide throughout the long adventure from our world to God's native country! The Spirit was there all along, whether we acknowledged Him or not!

I'm certainly not denying the challenges of this life. There are times of great challenge to our faith. We face many debilitating trials, but we are more than conquerors through Him Who loves us. Psalm 94:19 records the reflections of some ancient psalmist (and the words of God): "When anxiety was great within me, your consolation brought joy to my soul." Consolation is not an automatically "given." We must seek it *diligently* with our faith. "And without faith it is impossible to please God, because anyone who comes to him must believe that he exists and that he rewards those who earnestly seek him" (Hebrews 11:6). We can't expect consolation and rewards from God unless we put significant effort into it and earnestly seek Him.

Faith and Hope

Faith and hope are joined at the hip. True faith brings with it *true hope*. When hope begins to fade, we should check our level of *faith*, because they are inextricably joined together. I remember a man I consider to be a great encouragement in my life, Dr. M. Norvel Young, former president and chancellor of Pepperdine University. He accomplished a great deal in his life and overcame nearly insurmountable tragedies. I can still see the twinkle in his eyes as he said, "I stand on tiptoe to see what the future holds!" People gravitate toward a person with that kind of optimism. I loved Dr. Young dearly. Even when he was old, he would say, "The Bible doesn't say anything about retirement. God's heaven is our retirement!" True to his words, Dr. Young was working for Pepperdine (and the Lord) till the day of his death in his mid-80s. He was taken to heaven while he was in full stride!

Hope reaches into eternity. Hope actually sees the future and imagines the wonderful things that will someday be a reality. Hope is like a space probe that is launched from the platform of faith. It gives us vague, but real images of the future that move us forward.

If we have faith, we'll be convinced that what lies ahead

completely dwarfs what is present. Because there is always MORE. God promises that the future will not even compare to the here and now. Paul said, "I consider that our present sufferings are not worth comparing with the glory that will be revealed in us" (Romans 8:18). It's sometimes hard to believe, but you and I are going to be glorified someday! That means we'll be difficult to look at with human eyes, because we'll shine so brightly. I have heard story after story of people who sat at the bedside of a dying loved one, keeping vigil for the last moment, and being startled when the dying person rises up and says, "Oh my, I never dreamed it would be that wonderful!" And then dropping back, they depart for parts unknown.

But meanwhile, at this present time, God doesn't simply say, "Just endure till you are glorified in heaven." No, He wants us to be more than conquerors *here* and *now*. In God's view, life never really ends. We're simply changed from one degree of glory to another, until we are prepared for the spiritual world. He wants us to enjoy this present life abundantly and work for Him until He calls us home. We must not, cannot, give up. God may have our most productive days ahead of us, even though we're hurting, even though we are old or think we are useless. God specializes in recycling and using discarded things to bring glory to His Great Name. A devastated battlefield will one day be a beautiful meadow or a lush forest once again.

Norvel Young, whom I mentioned above and worked with at Pepperdine University, had another interesting saying with which he loved to encourage people: "The past is only prologue," he would say with a distant look in his eyes. His idea seemed to be that all that we have experienced is leading us to the future, when some wonderful thing will break in upon us. Dr. Young was thinking of more than heaven. He was thinking of what great things will happen *imminently*, in this life, to and by those who are used by God. I loved that.

How do we define life, anyway? In a real sense, life is *growth* and *change*. Many of us, of course, dislike both of those words! I remember people saying to me that they didn't believe they would live beyond their 20s or 30s. By the time they had reached their 40s and 50s, they realized that they had only begun, they had much more to contribute, more to accomplish, more to give their children and the world. Think of this: we spend a lifetime learning and accumulating knowledge, then we pass on into the next world. Is all that knowledge wasted; is it for nothing? Certainly not! I believe the Lord will use us and our accumulated knowledge in some higher purpose, either here or in His heaven. It's never a good time to give up on life and learning. Because there is always more.

It's Up to Us

When God creates us, He gives us an eternal soul. That soul is not simply physical breath, which will someday cease. It's some other substance called "spirit," supernatural life that will never die. The only thing to be decided is WHERE our future life will be spent—will we be in Christ or will we be cast outside of God's domain? *The choice is always up to us.*

Life is all about balance. We must learn to think *long term* as well as to think *short term*. What will we do with the eternal soul God has entrusted to us? The spirit He placed in our body is a precious gift that we often treat very lightly. Since God is an eternal Spirit, and since He created us in His own image, we too are eternal. The flesh will perish of course, because it's made only for this physical world. But the spirit lives forever because it's made for the next world. That's the nature of spirit—it exists forever. We just have to decide what we'll do with the spirit the Lord has given us. In a real sense, our long-term destination depends upon our short-term decisions. We must not think we're only floating in space with no purpose or destiny. We're meant for greater things. We're meant to do God's work, both in this realm and also in the next realm.

I'm amazed at how many people think we live in a material "closed system," a "box," with no input from outside the box and that everything is controlled by chance. No spiritual guidance. No morality other than what we ourselves invent. They believe they are under the control of a random toss of the dice—or something equally impersonal. I'm sure you know better than that. Actually, our sense of right and wrong is proof there is something beyond the closed system. No one can really explain where morality comes from—except, of course, "we invented it." Really?

God has you in the palm of His loving hand. He has great plans for you, no matter your age or your condition. You don't have to be blown by the wind of your every urge or feeling. Even if you have feelings of guilt or you are in despair at your present situation, regardless of how severe, there is more. You may be hurting, or alone, or just down in the dumps, but there is definitely more! Spring is coming … when you will spring into life again. Simply be open to the Spirit of God who will lift you up and make you stand. Romans 14:4 tells us that God will make us stand, because He is able—and He is willing. He wants to help and heal you.

With Brian Houston, I encourage you to believe "There is more." Make up your mind and determine to believe that nothing "in all creation will be able to separate us from the love of God that is in Christ Jesus our Lord" (Romans 8:39). With God's love beneath and covering you, you have great potential to bless others and to live a fulfilling life to the very beginning of the new age. It's never too late for you, because there is *always more!*

I will continue to fondly remember Dr. Norvel Young's famous statement: "I stand on tiptoe to see what the future holds!" I can see him rising up on his toes as he said that. Stir up your courage and your hope and look to the Lord. Because there's always more.

8

Spring Overcomes

The long winter is finally over. The tender green shoots of grass are there beneath the ice as it melts. The trees are budding, and everything is stirring to life. Spring is breaking through, and life is once again gloriously fresh and new!

I remember when I was living in Maine many years ago, how amazed I was at the coming of springtime in that cold environment of the North. It seemed that, for many weeks and months, the world would be grey and forlorn, frozen and unfriendly. Some days were brutally cold, down to 40 degrees below zero. I wondered, when will the welcome sun finally warm the earth again? But then, in a day or two, the snow would melt at an amazing speed. And there, beneath the cold white, would be beautiful green grass, looking as if it had always been there. The freshness and newness appeared, just below the freezing snow! It all seemed so sudden.

Like the renewal of life in springtime, God can suddenly overcome the chill of winter in our lives when we turn our face toward Him. He does that "springtime miracle" in our spirit and in our attitude. No matter how dark and dreary our world has become, the season of new life pushes up, pressing back the winter. It's then we learn that *Spring Overcomes!* What an extraordinary thing God does for us.

"This too shall pass" is an adage that has been around for many centuries. It appears to have originated in Persia, as some of their poets coined the phrase; then it was adopted into many languages around the globe. It's usually used in a sense of resignation, when people look at discouraging factors and shrug and say, "This too shall pass." It often seems to be about endurance, the idea being "This terrible or inconvenient thing has happened to us, but this too shall pass. We'll press on and win in the end."

But that's not the attitude I have in mind for this chapter. Here, we want to talk awhile about intensely watching for the coming of spring, watching for the thaw that brings new beginnings. I hope you understand that I'm using "spring" as a figure of speech.

Our lives are often in need of a springtime. So, the question we want to ask is, can we also LIVE in springtime continuously? In the first chapter, we talked about the coming of winter, with its bone-chilling cold. In the spirit realm, we know that tough times are bound to enter our life. But I believe we can overcome those times of doubt and disillusionment and pain. And there may be a way to live in newness of life—continuously—even when we're in the clutches of a bitter winter. I believe we can live as *overcomers*.

In past periods of pain, I've turned to contemporary praise or worship music. Perhaps you prefer the "old hymns." With due respect, maybe you should get over it! Certainly, there are time-honored hymns that will remain classics for ages to come, because of their great theology. But there are also hymns with archaic words and long-abandoned phrases that turn our minds backward. Some of those old hymns imply the past "good ol' days." I'm convinced that God wants us to move forward and recognize what He's doing NOW!

Psalm 98 begins with these words: "Sing to the LORD a new song, for he has done marvelous things; his right hand and holy arm have worked salvation for him." That psalm was written many centuries ago, but even then, the writer is calling us to "sing a new song." Why? Because God is a God of the NOW! He's not merely a God of yesterday's songs, but also of fresh, new songs with today's words and thoughts. God is not an old man with a long white beard sitting majestically in heaven. He's the dynamic, omnipotent force of the universe and beyond! Like a superhero but infinitely stronger, wiser, and bigger!

So, I like to listen to the contemporary worship songs of today, to remind me that God is *still* speaking to people, both young and old writers and composers, using the language and music of today. I'm deeply impressed by the spiritual themes of many of the "new songs" (not all songs, of course, to answer the complaints of older critics). I have found great consolation in the spiritual songs of today. Do we have to be careful about the theology of today's songs? Yes, of course, just as we have to be careful about some of the old hymns. We must not try to lock God into some specific era or epoch of time. Sing to God a *new* song!

The Overcomer

Jesus our Lord is the ultimate overcomer. In fact, He said, "I have overcome the world" (John 16:33). He made that statement in the context of telling us, "I have told you these things, so that in me you may have peace." We should do our best to remind ourselves: If we're allowing ourselves to be in the depths of despair, we're not trusting Jesus. He came to give us peace and hope. He said, "Do not let your hearts be troubled and *do not be afraid*" (John 14:27). He let us know that "troubled hearts" and "being afraid" were joined together. But for the believer, fear must be conquered, because it's really *the entrance of winter* into our soul. We desperately need the warmth of God's peace. The opposite of fear is faith.

Jesus had something far better than the world's idea of peace. He told us about *His kind of peace.* Jesus said, "Peace I leave with you; MY PEACE I give you. I do not give to you as the world gives" (John 14:27). So, there are definitely *two* kinds of peace: the kind the world gives, and the kind Jesus gives. Jesus is the great overcomer, even overcoming sin and death by His own death and sacrifice for sin. The Lord wants you and me to also be overcomers. Therefore, if Jesus grants us *His* peace, we should have a peace that cannot be comprehended. What kind of a peace is He talking about? He's talking about a *supernatural peace*, not merely a peaceful life in this world, or a peace that depends on material goods or one's welfare. But a confident peace that stretches out toward eternity. Supernatural peace can't really be defined. It's a profound confidence that covers us with protection and sets our heart free.

"Spring overcomes" is another way of saying, "We live in hope that things will be better soon." Because Jesus lives, we are assured that we too shall live. The Lord gives up the power to rise again—not the power from within us, to be sure, but power through the indwelling Spirit of God. It's evident that "evil days" will come into our lives. Or we might say, the freezing winter will probably chill our bones and our souls at one or more points in our lives. Those winters will probably come upon us unexpectedly. But because Jesus lives, we can overcome those bouts of depression and pain in His mighty name. When those evil days do come, you and I must run (not walk) to our Lord for His "springtime peace." So, we watch with eager eyes, searching, waiting for the first signs of spiritual springtime that are sure to come. Because winter is not a permanent condition; it's only a season that will pass.

Many individuals with limited spiritual insight see history going nowhere, with monotony and numbing sameness. But people of faith see history moving forward toward some climactic end, which will usher in the return of the Messiah. I think it's fascinating that in God's way of thinking and time keeping, things begin in darkness and finish in light. In the book of Genesis, the record of creation tells us, "the evening and the morning were the first day" (and the second and third day), and so on. Our world tends to think of morning as the beginning of the day, then the day ends with night. But what a difference it makes to envision darkness first, then light coming out of darkness! We're not moving toward the darkness; we're moving toward the light! Morning will break, and all things will be new. God has a very different concept in mind in which light conquers the darkness and springtime dispels the cold of winter.

God established cycles in the earth and in the universe. And those cycles always move our existence forward, rather than the way many ancient Asians viewed the cycles of life. For them, the Yin and the Yang simply revolved around, repeating endlessly, going nowhere. But we believe that history is definitely going somewhere, going toward some ultimate and perfect goal. The earth rotates; it makes its long orbit around the sun. Winter comes, *but spring overcomes.* The lowly caterpillar slowly climbs the tree and emerges later as a colorful butterfly—and *flies*, rather than crawls, away. This is our hope—that we're moving forward toward a beautiful, new life in a new realm, where we too will fly away.

The Yearning Heart

In Job 19:25-27, the embattled man who lived more than 4,000 years ago declared,

"I know that my Redeemer lives, and that in the end he will stand upon the earth. And after my skin has been destroyed, yet in my flesh I will see God; I myself will see him with my own eyes—I, and not another. How my heart yearns within me!"

Many of us know that same "yearning of the heart." Paul certainly did. He said, "Meanwhile we groan, longing to be clothed with our heavenly dwelling, because when we are clothed, we will not be found naked. For while we are in this tent, we groan and are burdened, because we do not wish to be unclothed but to be clothed with our heavenly dwelling, so that what is mortal may be swallowed up by life" (2 Corinthians 5:2-4). But while we are here in this life, we must wait a little longer. When winter comes, we should always look for the spring to follow. We wait and we yearn for God to ease our pain and loneliness. And He always heals us if we have faith.

In the middle of withering trials, Job had a confident hope of springtime! Winter swirled all around him, bitter sorrows were freezing his bones, but he had a living hope, faint though it was. Job believed in *metamorphosis*, the nearly miraculous change of form, shape, structure, and substance—complete transformation! Isn't it amazing that God gave us hints of transformation and new life even in this present existence? The tadpole, for example, begins its life as a fish, darting here and there beneath the surface of the water. But when it is fully developed, the tadpole becomes a frog, able to move from the water to the dry land: one more example of metamorphosis.

But the greatest example of this great transformation is the "new birth into Christ" in a person's life. From a mindless, uncaring human to *a child of the Living God*, there is a metamorphosis that's dramatic and stunning! The apostle Paul is an example of such a man who previously had his mind and heart set on violence, on persecuting and even killing followers of the Way. He did this in all good conscience, thinking he was actually doing the will of God. But in an instant, literally in the flash of bright light, he was changed and became the most important person in the history of Christianity, other than Jesus Himself. From Saul to the apostle Paul, he was completely changed.

In his day, Job couldn't see the future, and yet he proclaimed, "I KNOW my Redeemer lives ... yet in my flesh I WILL SEE GOD!" That's solid faith, in a day that was millennia before God had fully revealed Himself! And we can be sure that God will reward Job for his faithfulness. If we have that "Job kind of faith," we'll be able to proclaim with confidence, "Spring is coming!" Despite the loneliness and even in the teeth of defeat, we'll be able to say, "Spring overcomes all my pain, all my fear and all my loneliness." Truly, spring overcomes.

We can't manipulate the calendar and make spring come sooner. But *in the Spirit*, we can minimize the winter and hasten the coming of spring. When we're in the midst of winter and our minds are numb—and we have trouble praying—God understands. We can confess our true feelings and say, "God, I'm mad. I'm discouraged. I'm shaken. I'm finished!" No one can share our deepest feeling of aloneness or despair, except *God Himself.* He'll not chastise you and condemn you. Instead, Jesus will say, "Yes, I know, My child. I've been there, too. I was alone. I was abandoned and given over to a vicious mob. I hear your heart's cry. I'll be with you always."

New Life

Spring brings new life—a time to plant seeds and watch the new growth. Even in springtime, the planted seed must die in order for the plant to grow and produce good fruit. Jesus said, "But I, when I am lifted up from the earth, will draw all men to myself" (John 12:32). He expects us to plant the seed of our life, and to die to self, so that His new life will be created in us. Our life can become a great harvest through God's Spirit.

We've said that spring is a metaphor for new life. It's also a metaphor for the Spirit of God working in us. Jesus said, "When the Counselor comes, whom I will send to you from the Father, the Spirit of truth who goes out from the Father, he will testify about me" (John 15:26). Jesus asked the Father to send Holy Spirit to His people, to send *springtime* to the world! The Spirit is a *witness for Christ*, among His many other vital roles. How does that work? Remember that God sends the Spirit to live in us and be with us, and with the empowering of the Spirit, God's people share the good news about Jesus. *We're witnesses of Jesus*, because His Spirit (The Witness) testifies through us. And thus, spring comes to the world through us. Or more accurately, spring overcomes and the world has the opportunity for new life!

Many believers of the national fellowship to which I happen to belong are finally dealing with the whole idea of Holy Spirit. He is "The God I Never Knew," in the words of Robert Morris's book. Many old and staid denominations are coming alive with the renewed knowledge of the vital work of the Spirit of God. In the passage above, the Spirit is called "the Spirit of truth." Indeed, a critical truth that has often been lost is being rediscovered with wonderful results. People who have lost sight of the supernatural Spirit of Truth are being set free! We don't know all the many ways the Spirit works. But we must believe that Holy Spirit does indeed work in us and through us in this world.

So often we think that the good news of Jesus is shared through salesmanship, or argumentation, or extensive knowledge. We think we have to be an expert apologist, or marketer, or Bible scholar. But that simply is not true. The good news is shared through the honest, submitted heart of a believer who is called to be a witness for Christ. We must understand that we don't "witness" the way the earliest disciples and apostles testified to what they had seen and heard. But we can tell what

God has done for us, and that's witnessing.

Believers who welcome God's Spirit of Truth are issuing a sigh of great relief. The Ruach or Pneuma or Spirit of God is the "Sigh of God" (literally, the "wind" of God). As the Spirit of God sighs, so do the people of God. Spring is coming upon us! I urge you to call on, sigh for, Holy Spirit in the Name of Jesus!

I don't know about you, but for me, spring is the most glorious season of the year. I love it. Spring brings many memories to my mind. I think of several trips to the British Isles that I enjoyed with loved ones and friends, almost always in springtime. The cold and dreary snows and rains were past. The swollen streams of Wales gushed with sparkling melted snow. The Scottish Highlands were covered with grass and heather. The English farms, with never-ending sheep scattered across the landscape, and the cottages of the Cotswolds were glorious and breathtaking. I'll never forget the scenes of Britain's spring.

In winter, it's difficult to even think of spring. A few years ago, the Conejo Valley in Southern California, including the area where I lived, Westlake Village, was struck by a raging brushfire. The fire swept over the mountain from Simi Valley and burned many houses. It threatened the whole valley. At two in the morning, I was awakened and told to evacuate my home. It was a strange and lonely feeling as I drove on the empty freeway toward the south where my daughter lives.

God spared my house and many others, and the valley slowly got back to normal after several weeks. My point is, in a few months the grass had grown back and the trees had new leaves on them. Life had returned, just as it does every spring. But we couldn't even imagine that scene of green new growth in the early morning hours, in the red glow of the horrifying fire. Spring always returns, in a physical way and also in a *spiritual way*.

When Dark Times Come

The return of life—those are the pictures I try to bring to my mind when dark times come. But I also strain to "see the unseen," because there is a springtime of the spirit that can't be perceived with our human eyes. Ephesians 5:15-17 tells us, "Be very careful, then, how you live—not as unwise but as wise, making the most of every opportunity, because the days are evil. Therefore, do not be foolish, but understand what the Lord's will is." The Lord's will is yet another kind of energizing spring.

When "days of evil" come, it's amazing how quickly we can forget all the gracious leading and gifting of the Father. We're like people with dementia who don't remember the most recent of conversations or events; we're like people who can't even remember the names of their loved one. We are sympathetic toward those unfortunate people who, through no fault of their own, have lost their long-term, and even their short-term, memory. But what is our excuse when we forget the blessings of our God? Paul tells us to "be very careful how we live," not unwisely, but wisely "making the most of every opportunity."

Spring is when light overtakes the darkness. It's the vernal equinox when the days lengthen, and the warmth of summer is near. And spiritually, we wait for heavenly light to overtake darkness, evidence that spring is returning. What are we waiting for? We're waiting for the next thing from God; what astonishing thing will He do next? But we know this: whatever He does will be GOOD!

We can't afford to waste time living in the depths of winter. We're people of the springtime of the Lord. "Therefore, if anyone is in Christ, he is *a new creation*; the old has gone, the new has come!" (2 Corinthians 5:17). We're to live in newness, because we are new creations! Satan tries to convince us that we're the same old weak and sinful people we always were. But is that true? Are you no different than you were earlier in your life? Of course, it's not true, because you have been changed. It's one more lie from the father of lies. Who will we listen to, the liar or the one who loves us and gave His life for us? He says, "The long winter is over. Spring has come."

The world we live in is "the womb of heaven." Just as a mother's womb is a place of growth and preparation for the new life that's about to emerge, so this world is only the entryway to our true home. Don't fight against the birth that will deliver you to paradise. As C. S. Lewis said in a letter to Mary Willis Shelburne (who it is thought was dying), "Has this world been so kind to you that you should leave with regret? There are better things ahead than any we leave behind." Oh, how right he is! This world is a place of preparation.

I love the old song, "Morning Has Broken," written by Eleanor Farjeon in 1931 and set to the tune of a traditional Scottish Gaelic melody. A number of decades after Eleanor wrote the song, it became a popular secular song sung by folk singer Cat Stevens. It speaks of the "first morning" as a foreshadow of "every morning." The setting is from Genesis (the very beginning of things), but likened to our day.

> Morning has broken Like the first morning,
>
> Blackbird has spoken Like the first bird.
>
> Praise for the singing! Praise for the morning!
>
> Praise for them, springing Fresh from the Word!
>
>
> Sweet the rain's new fall Sunlit from heaven,
>
> Like the first dew fall On the first grass.

Praise for the sweetness Of the wet garden

Sprung in completeness Where His feet pass.

Mine is the sunlight! Mine is the morning

Born of the one light Eden saw play!

Praise with elation, Praise ev'ry morning,

God's recreation Of the new day!

When you're defeated, when guilt or loneliness surrounds you, when pain wracks your body, reflect on Eleanor Farjeon's thoughts of "freshness from the Word!"

Listen to the Lord's whisper, "My loved one, spring has overcome!"

9

God Is So Good

The most compelling reason to watch and wait for springtime is the truth that God is *so good!* He's not just "a little good," He's completely good! He is so, so good that we can't even imagine His goodness! Many of us allow our hardships to hide that wonderful truth from our eyes. But listen, that hiddenness can ultimately steal the divine escape out of life's hardships.

Think about this: "Then Moses said [to God], 'Now show me your glory.' And the LORD said, 'I will cause all my goodness to pass in front of you, and I will proclaim my name, the LORD, in your presence. I will have mercy on whom I will have mercy, and I will have compassion on whom I will have compassion. But,' he said, 'you cannot see my face, for no one may see me and live'" (Exodus 33:18-20).

Moses was asking, in effect, for the impossible. He wanted to see the glory of the Lord; the glory of God is in the "face" of God. But the glory of the Lord is far too brilliant for any human to ever see it or comprehend it. No mind can ever take it in. To see God's great glory, Moses would have to BE God, because only infinity can comprehend infinity.

So, instead, God said to Moses, "I will cause *all my goodness* to pass in front of you, Moses." How did God allow Moses to see Him? Since Moses couldn't possibly take in God's overpowering and unlimited glory, God said, "I will cause *all my goodness* to pass in front of you, and I will proclaim my name

[Yahweh] in your presence." Moses was not able to see the "glory" (the full manifestation of God) but he could see the "goodness"—at least PART of God's goodness.

The only way you and I can see God is to look at His *astounding goodness!* God is so good that we cannot even conceive of His goodness. The great friend of God, Moses, could look at only the "back side" of God's goodness, it was so remarkable. When we get just a glimpse of that goodness, it forever changes us. Only then will we be able to understand what omnipotence is.

It's not hard to be distracted from God's glorious goodness. We experience troubles that come our way—the discouragement, pain and loneliness—and we simply can't see "the forest for the trees." The enormous goodness of God gets lost in our immediate troubles, which are so minuscule by comparison. We begin to think the Lord is uncaring or unloving. We doubt His immeasurable goodness.

The Basis for Thanksgiving

The reason it's so vitally important to get a vision of the goodness of God is that understanding His goodness is *the basis* for our thanksgiving. If we don't truly grasp the depth of God's goodness, we may not offer Him our everlasting thanksgiving. As I survey my life from a distance of age, I see God there when I was a boy in the trauma of a world at war. I see Him as He spoke to a lonely little child, forced to play by himself in a dangerous world. I see Him encouraging me as a teenager who was unsure of his journey ahead. I did begin to understand His presence with me as I entered life in the Air Force and as I met my perfect wife-to-be, and then as we had our children, and as He led me to a rewarding life's career. And all I can manage to say is, "Hallelujah! Thank you, Lord, for

Your goodness, for the abundance of Your blessings in my life!"

Please understand that my life has not been without tragedies and heartaches. I've suffered times of crushing pain like everyone else. I'm no different than you. But somehow, God has helped me to not allow bitterness to seep into my life and poison my spirit. So, today I thank the Lord God for His unbelievable, incomparable goodness toward me! Indeed, where would I be, had it not been for the Lord? I can't imagine.

I've talked a lot about suffering, loneliness, and pain. That's because I've observed so much of those things in my own life and around me: scarcity, starvation, violence, kidnapping, enslavement, illness and loneliness.

But the truth is, for the great mass of people on earth, especially in America, most of life is good. Very good! Wouldn't it be amazing if the daily news boldly proclaimed, "Today, no one was hurt or killed or assaulted; no one was cheated today, no one was betrayed"? That would affirm that the usual news was horrible and the course of things was extremely terrible. It would suggest that what was unusual was to *not* have any tragedies!

Most of life is wonderful. I'm sure the majority of your life has been positive and enjoyable. But even when things are good, we've a tendency to take the good for granted. We need to be reminded that God doesn't owe us anything; if we are owed anything, we're due the penalty for our sinfulness. But thankfully, God doesn't give us what we deserve; He gives us what we don't deserve, and that's His amazing grace!

I love the part in *The Lion, the Witch and the Wardrobe*, by C. S. Lewis, when the Pevensie children stumble into Narnia and go to the house of Mr. Beaver and hear that "Aslan is on the move." "Who is Aslan?" asked Susan. Mr. Beaver explains that Aslan is the King, the "Lord of the whole wood." Then he explains that Aslan is not a man, but a Lion, the Great Lion! Lucy then asks the very important question, "Then he isn't safe?" Finally, Mr. Beaver says, "Course he isn't safe. But he's good. He's the King, I tell you.'"

Lewis, I believe, tells us something vital in that segment of the story. Like Aslan, Jesus is not safe; that is, we can't tame Him, somehow put Him in a box. He's the Lord, and we are the sheep of HIS pasture, not our pasture. On the other hand, Jesus is *absolutely good!* He is the good shepherd. He's the Great King, and He loves His sheep enough to die for them.

Keep in mind: Because of His triumphant sacrifice, Jesus holds the keys to death and Hades. Someday He will throw those two scourges into the Lake of Fire. They'll be utterly destroyed. The story will finally be finished, and we'll understand how we have been fitting into God's great drama. We'll know as we are known.

Meditating on the goodness of God works miracles for us. The old song, "Count Your Blessings," written in 1897 by Johnson Oatman, Jr., is a simple hymn with some archaic lyrics, but it contains valuable insights for us to consider:

> When upon life's billows you are tempest-tossed,
>
> When you are discouraged, thinking all is lost,
>
> Count your many blessings, name them one by one,
>
> And it will surprise you what the Lord hath done.

When you think about it, God has showered innumerable blessings on us. Typically, we ignore them, but we should "name them one by one," in the words of Oatman's hymn. When we're finished counting, "it will surprise you what the Lord has done." Gratefulness is a trait that the Lord appreciates in you and me. Meditating on the goodness of the Lord can generate deep gratitude toward Him, so that we say, "Indeed, God is so, so good!"

You may know the story of John Newton. He was a slave ship captain in the mid-1800s, who later was converted to the Lord Jesus. He could never quite get over the fact that God had forgiven him of his great sins. When he was old and his eyesight was failing, he would say, "Although my memory's failing, I remember two things very clearly: I am a great sinner and Christ is a great Savior." In my final days, my hope is that I have the presence of mind to make that same humble statement.

In perhaps the most beloved hymn of all time, "Amazing Grace," John Newton concluded his words with, "When we've been there ten thousand years, Bright shining as the sun, We've no less days to sing God's praise Than when we've first begun." Newton understood the tremendous value of faith that issues forth in highest praise to God.

Enter His Gates

In Psalm 100:4, 5, we're admonished to "Enter his gates with thanksgiving and his courts with praise; give thanks to him and praise his name. For the LORD is good and his love endures forever; his faithfulness continues through all generations." The psalmist of long ago affirmed that God is good, that His love endures forever, and that God's faithfulness goes on and on, through the ages. Even in heaven, we'll still be singing of His goodness, His love, and His faithfulness. Perhaps the perspective of heaven is the only definite experience that will elicit our overwhelming praise and honor for God.

God is so good that He has placed Jesus Christ at His right hand, next to Him on His exalted throne. Jesus is there now, where He was before His journey to earth 2000 years ago. In that privileged place, Jesus intercedes for you and me; He takes our requests to the Father and forgives our sins. *But there's more.*

We're told that, "God raised us up with Christ and seated us with him in heavenly realms in Christ Jesus in order that in the coming ages he might show the incomparable riches of his grace, expressed in his kindness to us in Christ Jesus" (Ephesians 2:6). That's a mouthful. But did you get it?

This passage is telling us that Jesus is on that throne with the Father, and we're seated *with Jesus* in the heavenly realms. That somehow puts us *on the throne* with Jesus and the Father! How can we understand that? We have to accept it by faith, of course, and if we do, it puts us in a remarkable position!

Here's the way I view that passage ... In my work with Pepperdine University, I used to attend elegant fund-raising luncheons and dinners. At those meals, the arrangers would often put name markers in each place, and guests would find their table, then walk around the table in search of the place markers with their name on it. The markers had been there for some time, maybe hours before, but only when the guest found his or her name marker was the seat actually filled. My understanding is that our place markers are already there at the table (and at the throne) in heaven, there at the right hand of God with Jesus. When we finally arrive in that heavenly realm, we only have to find our assigned place and claim it. So, there's a sense in which we are *already* seated there. Because our place is waiting for us, with *our very own* name on it, right next to Jesus!

To see the goodness of God we only have to look at His Son, Jesus Christ. Which is exactly what God hoped we would do, because Jesus is the very image of the invisible Father (Colossians 1:15)! The Lord Jesus never hurt or belittled a person, never led a rebellion, never gossiped or slandered anyone, nor, as Matthew said, "A bruised reed he will not break, and a smoldering wick he will not snuff out." He passed through this world without damaging anything. Instead, Jesus always was gentle and kind, always thoughtful and giving of Himself, always loved the lowly and the disenfranchised as well as those of wealth. The truth is, He was so good that the world couldn't stand Him and was intent on doing away with Him. His divine light was too bright for people to deal with, so they murdered Him. But the Father raised Jesus to life to die no more. Jesus was a portrait of the good Father.

God is so good that we simply cannot overestimate Him. In our wildest imagination, we can't envision the fullness and goodness of God. Every blessing of life—sight, sound, texture, sweetness and spiciness, love, satisfaction, rest, *everything*—is from the Father of Lights. From Him all blessings flow. All we know and all we experience is from God's endlessly fertile mind. He is our Great Creator! And the most wonderful thing is, He's not vindictive—He is good, only good!

Does God Punish Us?

"But," someone might object, "doesn't God punish people?" In fact, He disciplines people for their own good. He always hopes the discipline will bring people back to Him. And He gives them freedom to acknowledge Him or reject Him; He gives all of us choices, and we're free to choose death or choose life. We want our own children to have choices, but we wouldn't allow small children to play with knives and other dangerous things; we discipline them to save them from pain—because we love them. Just as God loves us. Our Father is infinitely more longsuffering than we, and He's not willing that anyone should perish.

God gives us laws and commandments, not to restrict us or

punish us, but to bless us by letting us know the *good* and *right* way. Think of a game, say football, that has no boundaries and no rules. It sounds ridiculous. Life without rules is impossible to live.

Because of our wickedness, many of us seem to despise God's instructions, even though they're meant to help us live happy and successful lives. A stubborn, rebellious heart is doomed to fall and fail. Jesus might say to rebellious people, "Seeing, they do not see; hearing, they do not hear." Many people just won't listen. But I'm sure that's not true of you. The very thought that you are reading these words puts you in a different camp. We can easily be weakened and slip away from our faith moorings; that's why the Lord calls us home for His forgiveness. So, in this last chapter, I want to encourage you and call you to a deeper commitment to Christ.

I'd like to remind you of where we've been in this book. In the first chapter, we talked of the coming of winter, about how heartaches and trials, illnesses and reversals, divorce and death can weaken our resolve to follow the Lord. Though we have the best of intentions, prolonged attacks of discouragement can chill our soul. Winter comes to every life.

The second chapter was about how seasons of suffering come to us like a wave, like repetitive *wave after wave*. The repetition often swamps us and takes us under. But we must brace ourselves against the onslaught and should run to God to help regain our balance and stand.

I particularly like chapter three that encourages us to "take heart." All is not lost, regardless of the devil's whispers. We have a Savior who loves us more than we know, a Savior who has overcome the world and offers us *His* kind of peace. We can be overcomers.

In chapter four, we thought specifically about the peace of

Christ and the tremendous difference it can make in our life. Jesus Himself is our Shalom, our divine peace. He was familiar with pain and suffering, but He purchased our pardon and freedom from guilt.

Chapter five encouraged us to look forward, not back. Trying to live in the past, rehearsing either good times or bad times, hinders healing. It's always a good thing to keep moving toward the future, because that's where our destiny is. God is the God of the future.

The suggestion that we get over and out of ourselves was the subject of chapter six. Self-focus can be a sort of prison that traps us into negative thinking and futile living. We should be thankful to the Father and live to help others, as Jesus did.

The seventh chapter was titled, *There Is More*, and the major thought was hope is eternal. Life is about change and the future. No matter what has happened in our life, there is always more. The final "more" is in God's heavenly "home country."

Chapter eight completed the thoughts of chapter one (*The Coming of Winter*) with the assurance that *spring eventually overcomes* if we hold on and never give up. Times of refreshing always come from our loving Father. We should look to Him for the power to rise!

The Final Thought

And now we come to this final chapter. The truth, the realization, that will change our lives and change specific situations is, *God is so good!* That's a knowledge that comes from trusting Him and proving Him to be faithful. We read about that in the eternal Word, which the Lord has given us. The overarching truth of the Scriptures is, God is good, and He wants only good for His creation, even the inanimate material creation, this physical world. He told us in Romans 8:19-24,

> The creation waits in eager expectation for the sons of God to be revealed. For the creation was subjected to frustration, not by its own choice, but by the will of the one who subjected it, in hope that *the creation itself* will be liberated from its bondage to decay and brought into the *glorious freedom* of the children of God. We know that the whole creation has been groaning, as in the pains of childbirth right up to the present time. Not only so, but we ourselves, who have the first fruits of the Spirit, groan inwardly as we wait eagerly for our adoption as sons, the redemption of our bodies. For in this hope we were saved.

That passage is worth meditating upon for some time. It's telling us that we're not the only ones who are in a struggle. *All of creation* is decaying and groaning—and waiting for our "adoption as the children of God." Those words hint that this beautiful world (the creation that God repeatedly called "good" in Genesis 1) will not be completely lost, but will be liberated and will be "brought into the glorious freedom of the children of God."

Have you marveled at a sunlit ocean, or a distant mountain range, or a sweeping desert landscape, or a lush evergreen forest? I know you have. You may someday see those things again in the next world, only they will be more beautifully presented, in God's native country.

God is so, so good! Believe it! Our Father has nothing evil or ugly in Him—at all. He's beautiful through and through! He knows every one of us intimately. If we only knew His true self, Oh, how we would love Him!

He knows you and calls you by name! He wants to be a

Father to you, a Friend to walk with you as you head to your true home. He's the ultimate source of all things good—because He's the good, good Father.

We simply don't have time for negative feelings or thoughts. Leave pain and suffering, disappointment, and discouragement behind. We are children of the Living God!

Amen.

Epilogue

As I look back over many years, I'm truly overwhelmed by the goodness of God. I believe that even that wonderful conclusion is a gift from our gracious Lord.

The tragedies, defeats, and pains of my life vanish away in the Light of His searing love and goodness. I've learned to press toward and bask in His Light, rather than linger in the darkness that tries to insinuate itself into my mind and heart. It has been a remarkable journey toward eternal life. I wish the same for you, my friend.

To dwell on the evil, the untrue, the ugly and, yes, even the past, can cause us to live in that dreadful place continually. Why would we ever do that? I've found we sometimes go to that place because there's a force that supernaturally draws us there, like a moth to the flame. It's a sinister force whose only goal is to steal, kill, and destroy. I pray you will choose Jesus and the heavenly Father, the *Life and Light*, rather than the destructive *flame of the enemy*. Because, it's God's unfathomable love that lifts us to Him—upward toward the Light of Jesus, God's Son. Someday we will live in that Light continually, forever. I pray I'll meet you there.

Bill Henegar

May 2020

CPSIA information can be obtained
at www.ICGtesting.com
Printed in the USA
LVHW010528211220
674732LV00010B/285

9 781647 734008